I0455483

The Prepper's Bundle
Even More Survival Guides for Every Situation

By Robert Paine

© 2014

Table of Contents

The Prepper's Bundle: Even More Survival Guides for Every Situation

Sign up for Robert's Mailing List to be notified of **New Releases** and **Special Sales**: http://eepurl.com/zvm11

Other Books by Robert Paine:
The Ultimate Prepper Collection: Survival Guides For Every Situation
Prepper's Pantry: A Survival Food Guide
The Survivalist Cookbook - Recipes for Preppers
Prepping 101: A Beginner's Survival Guide
The Dead Road: The Complete Collection

Bugging Out or Bugging In?

Introduction

There are plenty of guides that tell you all about bugging out and what to do if you need to bug in, but this guide will cover each option in depth. You will find checklists of items you will want to get together to make bugging in or bugging out work for you and your family. There are plenty of tips, tricks and best practices to help you be successful in your goal to be prepared for nearly anything. You will find everything you ever needed to know about storing food, water and other necessary supplies.

This is the kind of guide you will reference often as you pack your bug out bag and stockpile food and water. There are so many factors to consider when it comes to prepping it is easy to overlook a small, but very important detail. This book is meant to guide you through every aspect of prepping while providing you with ideas and options you can apply to your life and where you live.

What is Bugging?

If you have an interest in survival and prepping, you have probably heard the term "bugging out" or "bugging in" quite a bit. It is essentially what prepping is all about. So, what is it? The term bugging was originally used by military personnel. When things became too dangerous for troops and other military personnel to remain in a location, they would bug out. Meaning, they got out of an area before there was an invasion or attack. Now, if you want to get really technical, the phrase is rumored to have stemmed from actual bugs scattering from a location, but that cannot possibly be proven. Another theory is the British military used the term buggered out and the Americans quickly picked up on it. From there, civilians have begun using the term in prepping circles.

Bugging is the act of surviving the aftermath of an event that leaves the world as you know it upside down and inside out. If you have read blogs or other eBooks about survival and prepping, you have probably seen the terms, TEOTWAWKI and SHTF. The first stands for The End Of The World As We Know It and that last is a little more vulgar and stands for when S*** Hits The Fan. When one or both of these things happen, your bugging plan goes into motion.

If you haven't taken the time to prepare, the hours and days following a major event can be overwhelming. It can be extremely devastating to your state of mind, which survivalists will tell you is a huge concern. Your mind is a powerful tool. Imagine the comfort you will feel knowing you have food, water and medical supplies when the rest of your neighborhood has been turned upside down. Although you will still have a lot on your plate, marking off the necessities of life can make a dire situation, tolerable.

People who have taken the time to learn about what is needed to survive an event are referred to as preppers. Prepping to live seems pretty natural, but many are still not on board. When you add the word bugging to the equation, people really get uncomfortable. However, for those who understand what it means, it is actually a little comforting knowing you are prepared to bug in or bug out.

What's the Difference Between Bugging In or Bugging Out

You understand the idea of "bugging," but how do you know when it is time to leave the comfort and safety of your home or other location and head out for the open wilderness, forest or whatever the surroundings? Bugging out is setting out with whatever you can carry on your back or in some cases, in your car. This is always going to be a decision that needs to be made hours or days before an impending event. If you feel like your location is secure enough for you to bug in, that will be the focus of your preps.

City dwellers and those that live in the suburbs often plan to bug out to a secret location where they will bug in for the duration. Bugging out involves carrying a single or several bags that have been packed ahead of time. The bags are filled with the necessities you need to survive in the outdoors.

If you know your home is not a suitable place to try and ride out a major storm, a terrorist attack or other catastrophic event, you need to make plans to bug out. The moment you see a major storm headed your way or the moment you know an attack is imminent, it is time to bug out if the safety of your home will be compromised. Now, depending on the scenario, you may only need to bug out to a hotel or a relative's home in a neighboring city or town. It is impossible to predict with accuracy what kind of situation you will be faced with.

On the flip side of that, if things are going downhill in a hurry, you need to do what is necessary to secure your home to bug in. If it isn't safe to leave or you don't think you can make it to another location without encountering danger, bugging in is usually the best bet. When you are in your own home, you have those creature comforts you have come to love and appreciate.

Every family will have to make the decision based on the circumstances. Later in the book, we will discuss the things that you need to do to prepare for either scenario. Every prepper knows you have to be ready to deal with almost anything. Putting all your "eggs" in the bugging in basket could be extremely dangerous. You just never know when an attack is going to hit your home. You also don't know if you will be able to safely bug out when the time comes. You need your home to be stocked enough to keep you and your family alive until it is safe to bug out.

The old saying, "The best laid plans of mice and men often go awry," can and should be applied to prepping. You just never know.

Common Reasons for Prepping

In the survival world, you will find a wide number of reasons given for why people are getting involved in the prepping movement. You could ask 20 different preppers the same question and you are likely to get 20 different answers. The reasons people decide to start prepping vary widely, but the goal is always the same—to survive a catastrophic event.

The following are just a few of the reasons people choose to prep.

- War on our soil
- Civil unrest
- Terrorist attack
- Natural disaster i.e. hurricanes, earthquakes, severe storm
- EMP—electromagnetic pulse from the sun
- Pandemic
- Worldwide economic collapse
- Personal comfort in case of job loss, family tragedy
- Religious reasons
- Major climate change

Your reasons may be all of the above or something totally different. Ultimately, if you are prepping for a specific event, like a pandemic, your preps may be a little different than somebody who is prepping for a major financial collapse. No matter your reason for prepping, it is always done with the same goal of surviving. Parents tend to make up a majority of the prepping population. It is instinct to want to protect your children and that includes helping them survive situations that could otherwise be life-threatening.

Preppers have taken the initiative to prepare for a disaster because it is highly likely there will not be help readily available in the aftermath. When there is some catastrophic event, it could take weeks or even months before there is any relief. You have to be able to survive on your own without the luxury of having a store to run to or the ability to call 911 or receive government assistance. Many people do not fully understand what it is like to truly be on their own. We have become so accustomed to getting everything we need at a store or calling for help, it will be a major adjustment for everybody. Those who have prepared will even struggle a bit to come to terms with the situation. People who didn't prepare are going to be devastated.

They are going to be forced to do things they may have never considered in the past just to survive. That does not bode well for society. Crime will likely be out of control as people become savage in their search for food, water and critical medicines. With no law to regulate those who are killing and thieving, it will be a very rough world.

Although preppers tend to be a quiet bunch who don't like to talk a lot about what they have (for good reason), you will find there are plenty who would prefer it if the entire population did their own prepping. It would make things much more civilized if everybody had their own food stores to turn to. Unfortunately, that isn't the case and the majority of the population will scoff at the idea of stocking up on food and water.

Bugging Out

Bugging out is something that requires careful consideration. If you are leaving the safety and comfort of your home and heading off into the forest, desert or whatever the terrain, you cannot afford to forget a single item. One single tool could mean the difference between life and death. If bugging out is your plan when things go sideways, it is important to make sure the whole family is prepared to survive without the comforts of the home. You would be doing yourself a major disservice if you were to haphazardly run through the home tossing things in a bag that you think will help you survive in the minutes before or after a disaster. It would likely send you off into the wild blue yonder with a false sense of security. When it came time to set up a shelter or procure water, the large amount of food and your toothbrush are not going to help you.

It takes a great deal of planning to pick and choose the right items to put in the bug out bag. You should also spend some time packing the bag carefully. The more organized your packing job, the more stuff you will be able to fit in. When you are forced to act in haste, your decision-making suffers.

What is a Bug Out Bag

In order to bug out, you need a bug out bag. This is the bag that is going to keep you alive. In a serious catastrophe, everything you own in life could very well be in that bag. Without stores or somewhere to buy supplies, what you pack in your bug out bag will be all that you have to carry you through a disaster.

A bug out bag is a backpack filled with key tools that will aid in survival. The bag is going to hold your food, water and various tools needed to get more food, clean water and build a shelter. The bags are packed and ready to grab when it is time to bug out. When you have a bug out bag, you don't have to spend precious minutes deciding what to pack and shove it into a bag haphazardly. If you go this route, you can pretty much guarantee you are going to forget something important.

Every prepper and survival expert knows the key to staying alive and making it through a disaster situation is a well-stocked bug out bag. Our military carries backpacks into the field in case they are not able to make it back to camp. These bags are essentially their survival packs. A bug out bag is basically the same thing, but used by civilians. Our military has come up with some pretty awesome ideas and preppers are constantly integrating them into their own lifestyles and preps. With all the experience and hands on training in the military, it is safe to say what works for them will work for civilians. There is no need to try and reinvent the wheel so to speak. Learn from them and you will save yourself a lot of time and energy.

Picking the Right Bag

Bigger packs are not always better. Take some time picking out a backpack that you can wear comfortably. Ideally, framed packs are your best bet. You have the option of choosing from an internal frame or an external frame. In many ways, they are equal. However, external frames tend to be a bit heavier. There is some new technology that has made external frame packs a little lighter, but unless you are willing to spend a great deal of money on one of these packs, your best bet is an internal frame.

Framed backpacks are ideal because they spread the weight of the pack across your hips and take some of the pressure off your back and shoulders. You can also get a lot more supplies in a framed pack. The downside to the framed packs is their cost. They can be very expensive, upwards of $300 for a good, sturdy pack. You can often find the packs at secondhand stores and online. However, you want to inspect the pack carefully to ensure the stitching is still tight and your goods are not going to fall out as you climb a hill.

If you are opting to go with a standard backpack, make sure it has adequate shoulder padding, lots of pockets inside and out to maximize space and is not made of a material that is prone to shredding. Wide straps are ideal. When the backpack is loaded down, you don't want thin straps that will dig into your shoulders as you walk. A hip belt is a very important accessory. It will keep the pack positioned on your back so it isn't flopping around when you are walking and climbing. You need to be able to maintain your balance and a shifting backpack will impede your ability to move. A sternum clip is nice, but not necessarily a necessity. It further anchors the pack to your body by maximizing the chest bone.

Yet another concern is the material that will be against your back. You will want to choose a bag that has a mesh or breathable lining that will be against your body. While it will still be hot and you will likely still sweat a little where the pack rests against your body, you don't want it to be overly hot. This will create chafing and be uncomfortable in general. The breathable material will allow for some airflow to reduce the majority of the sweating.

You also should avoid brightly colored packs. If you are bugging out, chances are you don't want to stand out like a sore thumb. You want to be able to blend into your surroundings. Higher quality packs are worth the extra cost. A flimsy bag will not be able to withstand a lot of wear and tear. You need something that is rugged and durable. Because the bag is going to hold your life in it, it is a wise decision to make the investment to buy at least one really good bag. You can buy a few other bags that are of a lesser quality to keep on hand for family members to pack out.

Pick a bag that has lots of loops, straps and zippered pockets that allow you to hang things from the outside of your bag. Outside, zippered pockets are ideal. These allow you to store things that you need quickly and most often, like flashlights, water purification methods and a knife. Zippers keep gear where it is supposed to be. Invest in what the military refers to as MOLLE clips. These are clips that you hang from the outside of your pack and are used to hold gear you need in a hurry. The clips detach from the bag with a simple snap, which allows you to reach critical gear quickly without digging through your bag or unzipping pockets. Your whistle is best left hanging from your bag as is a flashlight or canteen.

Newer bags that have been designed for hikers have camelbacks integrated into the pack. These are luxurious! You can carry water without packing around a heavy bottle. A camelback is a flat bladder that would sit across your back. A straw is connected and brought over your shoulder for you to sip on when you get thirsty. These are ingenious and oh so valuable in a bug out situation.

Size matters when choosing a bag for each member of the family. REI has created a chart for you to use to help you determine what size of bag will fit best on your body. The length of your torso will determine which pack is right for you. See below.

Pack Size	Torso Length
Extra Small	Up to 15 ½ inches
Small	16 to 17 ½ inches
Medium/Regular	18 to 19 ½ inches
Large/Tall	20+ inches

Some people will opt to use a duffel bag, but this is generally not a good idea. They are not easy to carry. While you can certainly pack a lot more gear in a duffel bag, they are just obnoxious to try and carry over rough terrain.

What to Pack in Your Bug Out Bag

This is probably the most important bag you will ever pack in your life. It requires careful consideration and planning. Unfortunately, you can't pack everything, including the kitchen sink. You are going to be carrying this bag on your back and cannot afford to pack it so full it becomes a major burden. A bag that is heavier than you can pack with ease will hinder you and can cause you to trip, fall or be unable to move as fast as you need to. There is a fine line between packing too much and packing enough to survive. Bigger packs are not always better. While some burly men are okay carrying 70 pounds on their backs, the general population is not cut out for that. As you pack your bag, you are going to want to weigh it on your bathroom scale and test it out on your own back.

The following list includes the things you absolutely must have in your pack. Another list will outline some additional items that can make life a little easier, but are not necessarily crucial to your immediate survival. Keep in mind, these supply lists are made with the idea of sustaining one to two people. If you are bugging out with your family, you will want to create bug out bags for each member. In the next section, we will discuss the process of creating a bug out bag for a child—yes, they need one!

Essential Bug Out Bag Supplies

- Water purification method; tablets, filtration straws, portable filters
- Fire starting method—at least 2 ways; waterproof matches, lighter, magnesium stick, flint rod and steel
- Cordage i.e. paracord, rope
- Canteen or collapsible water bottle
- Good quality knife
- Poncho
- Trash bags—these have numerous uses i.e. water containment, ground barrier, poncho and etc…
- 2 Mylar survival blankets—these aren't meant to keep you warm necessarily, but make an excellent heat shield and can keep you dry. Choose high quality blankets when possible.
- First aid kit—see next section for what to pack
- Folding shovel

- Headlamp—LEDs are best, lightweight and last longer than a typical flashlight
- Wool socks
- Work gloves
- Compass
- Whistle
- Energy bars
- Insect repellant
- Sunscreen
- Chapstick
- Medications you need for survival
- EpiPen if you have one

Those are the bare minimums. The next list you can pick and choose from based on your personal needs and preferences.

- Sleeping mat
- Personal hygiene i.e. toothpaste, toothbrush, soap, toilet paper
- Feminine hygiene products
- Wet napkins
- Washcloth-compact cloths that are about the size of a 50-cent piece are perfect
- Tinder bundle material
  - Lint from the dryer

- o Dried moss
- o Cotton balls soaked in Vaseline
- o Dried grass
- Multi-tool—Swiss Army knife
- Tarp
- Wool blanket
- Change of underwear
- Freeze-dried food packs
- Portable stove—mini burners
- Metal cup
- Hand crank radio—battery powered is optional, but batteries are heavy
- Duct tape
- Self-defense i.e. gun, knife, Taser, pepper spray
- Ziploc bags for storing supplies, keeps bugs out and gear dry
- Backpack cover to keep pack dry
- Fishing line and hooks
- Super glue—serves a number of purposes and can be used to close wounds
- Sewing kit
- Bandana—used for signaling or covering the face to block dust or keep warm
- Light sticks

First Aid Kit list

The following list will help you put together a first aid kit to store in your bug out bag. Keep in mind; this is meant to be a personal use kit. You can certainly give out a band-aid or two, but your supplies are going to be limited so use cautiously. You will want to store your first aid kit in a small pouch or large Ziploc bag. For small kits, pencil cases work great for keeping all of your medical supplies together. You could also use makeup bags that are clear. This makes it easy to see what you need. Hard cases tend to be heavier. Gauze will still work, even if it is a little smashed. You could ensure your first aid supplies stay dry by putting them in a small case and then putting the case in the large Ziploc bag.

- 2 2x2 gauze pads 2 4x4 gauze pads
- Medical tape
- 4 band-aids in each size, small, medium, large
- Gauze roll—remove from box and put in small sandwich bag to save space
- 4 pain reliever tablets i.e. ibuprofen/acetaminophen
- 2 packs of aspirin
- Triple antibiotic cream
- Alcohol wipes
- Mole bandages for blisters
- Butterfly stitch bandages
- ACE bandage
- Latex gloves—2 pair minimum

- Antihistamine tablets—Benadryl
- Pepto-Bismol tablets—stop diarrhea, which could lead to dehydration
- 2 absorbent compress dressings—feminine napkins work great!
- Tweezers
- Medical scissors
- Iodine
- Garlic tablets—garlic is a natural antibiotic and can help fight an infection when there are no antibiotics
- Small book that outlines basic First Aid

Do not get carried away with your first aid kit. Your bug out bag and accompanying first aid kit are meant to get you from point A to point B. The kits are not meant to be a complete kit that can be used to do surgery in the field—if you even knew how to do that. If you have a bug out location in mind, store your major medical supplies there.

A note about water filtration devices:

There are plenty of different options on the market to clean water. However, you must realize you need something that is portable and will last longer than a single use. Tablets are easy and fairly quick to use, but when they run out, what will you do? Filters are excellent as well, but again, after filtering so many gallons of water they are ineffective. Boiling is one of the only constants you have, which is why a cup or pot is important to have. You need to be able to heat your water to kill off pathogens.

When you are shopping for your water cleaning tools, there are two main kinds, filters and purifiers. They are not the same.

Filters - Filters are removing visible impurities and the majority of bacteria that may be in the water. Filters do NOT remove most viruses from the water. Filters are a physical barrier, like charcoal or a cloth that the water passes through. You need to choose a filter that filters up to .02 microns. This means the filtering system catches the tiniest germs and bacteria that may be in the water.

Purifiers - Purification is chemically treated water that effectively kills bacteria, viruses and neutralizes most chemical contaminants. However, if you know a body of water is filled with fertilizer run off, it is best to avoid it altogether. Bleach or iodine are the best ways to purify your water. Those little tablets you are packing in your emergency preps are purifiers. If you are dealing with water that has some floaties in it, run it through your bandana before dropping a tablet in.

Some people will pack along charcoal tablets to create their own filters. This will work. You could also use charred wood from a campfire or burned out tree if necessary. Charcoal grabs onto bacteria and traps it when water is run through it.

Bug Out Bags for Kids

The kids need their own bug out bags. This will help you ensure you have enough supplies for the whole family and takes advantage of every available person to help carry supplies. Everybody needs to pull their weight in a survival situation. While you don't need to load the kids up with a bag quite as big as yours, you still want to make sure it is filled with the essentials. You will also want to choose a bag that is a bit smaller and fits the child. Refer to the chart above. An overly large bag could make it difficult for a child to walk and even cause trips and falls. A fall in a survival situation is much more serious. There isn't an emergency room to run to if the child breaks an arm or splits their lip open. It can be a little difficult to find a plain child's bag in a subdued color, but look around and check the internet. You don't want your little girl carrying a bright pink Hello Kitty backpack that will stand out in a copse of trees.

The list of supplies in the first essential list can be packed into a child's backpack with room to spare. Use common sense when it comes to stocking large knives in a child's bug out bag. It isn't necessary for the child to carry a foldable shovel as well if you have one. Use your best judgment when packing bags for kids under the age of about 12. Some kids are better prepared to use the gear you are packing. If you trust your 6-year-old to carry matches, than go for it.

When you pack bug out bags for young kids, you are doing so with the intention of them being with you or another adult with an adequately stocked bug out bag. However, you also want your child to be able to survive if they get lost or have to set out on their own. This would be in extreme situations, but in the midst of a serious crisis, things do tend to be extreme. Some people distribute supplies among the family in somewhat of a divide and conquer approach. This is a great idea if the entire family is traveling together, but if one person has the fire starting material and another has the water purification tablets and the group gets separated, all of the bug out bag planning in the world isn't going to make that situation any better. Every bag should have the basic necessities. Spread out the extra, non-essential gear if you would like.

When you think about it, having all the extra gear when you do reach your destination is a boon. Instead of having a couple bags of waterproof matches, you will have close to 10 or however many you pack in each of your family member's bags.

If you have a teenager who drives or may be at work or school when things get crazy, you will want them to be able to make it to a designated location as well. You can typically count on a teenager knowing how to use a knife effectively as well as the remaining gear. Discuss each piece of gear in the bag with your teen before it is ever actually needed. Have the teen keep the bag in their car.

In many cases, your kids are not going to want to carry around two backpacks - one for school and one for their survival gear. It just won't work. Keep a bug out bag at home for your child and create a small kit they can keep in the bottom of their school backpack. Those little pencil pouches are excellent for a few key pieces of survival gear as well. Toss in a bag of water purification tablets, waterproof matches, Mylar blanket, and a multi-tool. This is best for a child that is responsible enough to leave the gear alone and not "play" with it. Those few necessities can keep them alive until you get to them or they get to you.

A well-stocked bug out bag is great, but if you have never used the gear and are not familiar with it, it will do you little good in a survival situation. Spend some time at least once a month working with the gear with the kids. Trying to start a fire in the rain isn't easy, especially when trying to use a magnesium stick. It is a skill that requires practice. You can save yourself some money by purchasing quality gear that can be used repeatedly. Training in a survival situation is not ideal and could ultimately cost lives. Take a hike or go out on a campout with the kids and practice! Teach them about the tools they have in their bags and when they would want to use each tool.

Where to Store Bug Out Bags

A bug out bag will be worth more than a truckload of gold in a serious crisis. You will want to protect it and hide it from those who will be willing to kill you to take it from you. When the world is in chaos, people do things they normally wouldn't do. Your next door neighbor may suddenly become your biggest enemy if he wants and needs what you have to help his family survive. There is no law and there will certainly be no order as your friends, neighbors and co-workers all fight to survive. Those who haven't prepared are going to be coming straight for your front door if they know with certainty you have gear that will keep them alive.

You need to stash your bug out bag in a location that is safe and secure, but easily accessible by you and your family members. Sticking it by your front door for all visitors to see is not a good idea. If you plan on guests coming over for a barbecue or to watch the game, just use common sense when it comes to leaving your gear in plain view. People get curious and they will ask questions. While you certainly want to discuss the topic of having a backup plan and what people can do to prepare, you definitely don't want to advertise what you have.

The back of a closet, behind some food in a pantry or in an old bucket in the garage are all good places to hide your bag. Some people get creative and hide their bag in crates that are masked as furniture. A wooden box makes a great place to hide a couple of bags. Cover the crate with a pretty tablecloth; add some knick knacks or a lamp and guest will never realize what they are looking at. The idea is for you to know exactly where the bags are and be able to reach them quickly. Don't get too carried away with your hiding tactics. If you have to use a hammer to pull of sheetrock or tear into a floor to get to your bag, it defeats the purpose.

It is a really good idea to have more than a single bug out bag. You never know when a disaster could destroy your home and your survival gear with it. Ideally, you will want to have a bag in your car as well. Hide it under a blanket in the backseat or in the trunk. Many cars have a small space under the floor of the trunk. This is a great place to stash a small bag. A bag in an outdoor storage shed in case your home is destroyed gives you another layer of protection. It is always better to be over prepared than under.

Check out some of the other places you can hide your bug out bags.

- In a rubber tote marked "Christmas decorations. Throw a strand of lights and garland over the top, just in case somebody looks.
- Inside a box in a closet marked, "winter clothes" or something along those lines
- At the bottom of a garbage can in the garage or on the porch. Put a liner in the can and add a few bits of trash.
- A hollowed out area under a stairwell, camouflage the area with a rug or hang a picture if it is in a wall

You will want to get creative with your own hiding spots. Just remember to keep the bug out bag somewhat accessible so you can grab it in a hurry. You will also want your family members to know where it is at and how to get to it should they be in charge of retrieving the bug out gear. There are times when you won't be home or you could be injured. There are some places you don't want to put your bug out bag. Hiding your bag in a place that can cause your gear to become damaged will defeat your purpose of survival.

- Areas that are prone to wetness i.e. under kitchen sink, on the floor in basement

- Avoid areas that are prone to extreme heat—this can degrade things like your food supplies and Mylar blanket. Ideally you want a place that has an average temperature of 80 degrees or less.
- Avoid areas that are prone to extreme cold—outdoor sheds in areas where the temperatures drop below 10 degrees is not a good idea.
- Keep the bag out of direct sunlight

Bugging In

If leaving your home is not the best plan for you and your family, you need to plan to hunker down and weather whatever catastrophe has stricken your area. This is probably the ideal thing to do for most. There are numerous benefits to staying in your own home in an area you are familiar with. Maybe you have like-minded neighbors who will be able to offer support. Small communities provide normalcy and can help make an area a bit safer.

However, if you live in the middle of a city, hunkering down after a major disaster isn't always a good idea. A heavily populated area will mean more people trying to survive on little to no supplies. Those people are going to come looking and your home may be compromised. With that said, there is a lot to be said for bugging in. It gives you the chance to create a healthy stockpile of food, water and of course, it provides you shelter. Being able to stay in your own home also provides a level of comfort and security that is vitally important in uncertain times. There are many preppers who essentially prepare for the worst—bugging out, but hope for the best—bugging in.

If you only need to ride out a storm or some similar event that will be over in a matter of days, staying home is usually the best idea. The government often advises people to do this. It is safer to stay inside, with your head down so to speak. Wait to leave the house until you hear it is safe to do so.

What to Store for Bugging In

When you think about bugging in, it can be a bit overwhelming. This section will break it down into easy to swallow bite size pieces. Keep in mind, you don't want to run out and max out your credit card trying to buy everything you need to keep your family alive for a year. Be frugal and buy food items when they are on sale. Do some shopping around to compare prices. Buying online is usually going to be your best bet, but there are often closeout sales in local business that can save you money on shipping.

You need to assume you are going to be living in your home without access to outside food, water and other supplies. What you have in your home when disaster strikes is what you will have to live on. There are a lot of different considerations you will have to think about when planning to bug in. You have to plan on taking care of your entire family for days or even months. Be prepared to do a little math as you determine how much food and water you need to store. If you are new to the idea of prepping, it is helpful to start small. Begin with stores to last 30 days. Once you have that, build up to 3 months and then 6 months and finally, a year's worth of food. In a way, you can think of it as preparing to run a marathon. You need to do some training first before you jump in with both feet.

Food

Your food storage should be enough to last at the bare minimum 3 days. That is the very lowest you should ever have on hand at any given time. Ideally, you should stock enough food to feed your family for about 30 days. Available space, funds and your personal desires will dictate how much food you ultimately store. As mentioned above, you will need to ease into. Don't ever stop prepping once you reach your goal of 30 days or whatever you have decided upon. It is something that is always at the forefront of your daily life. If you come across a sale that has tuna fish at .50 cents a can, by all means by 20 if you have the money. If you already have a healthy stockpile of tuna in your food stores, it doesn't matter. The more food, the better.

Food stores are not about providing enough food for the family to eat until they are full. It is about providing enough food to keep the family going strong. It is more about the calories than the actual amounts. Don't get too hung up on calorie count and try to get by with the bare minimum. There is a rule in survival prep—You can never have too much food!

Here are some facts about the amount of calories you need to survive.

*Count on an average of 2500 calories per person

*You will burn more calories in a survival situation as you chop wood, hunt, carry water and garden

*Young men will need upwards of 4000 calories to maintain their strength

*Women need fewer calories—approximately 2,200

*Children will need about 1,400 calories a day

*While you can technically go 3 weeks without eating, you will become weak, lethargic and lose muscle mass within days of not eating

Using the assumption that you want to store about 2,500 calories a day per person, use the following formula for each member of the family over the age of about 13.

2,500 x number of people in home x number of days=the amount of food.

You will need to pay attention to the labels on the food you are storing. For example, a freeze-dried meal of chili provides 400 calories per serving.

There are 16 servings in a can. 16 x 400=6,400 calories in a single can.

6,400 calories divided by 2,500 calories per person=2.5 days of food for a single person.

This will give you an idea of the amount of food we are talking about when talking about storing for a month. Of course these are just examples and many of the freeze-dried foods will have higher calorie content. This is meant to give you a real idea about the amount of food it takes to keep a family of 4 alive for a month.

Many people get into a false sense of security when they start buying those cans of freeze dried meals. It looks like a lot when it is sitting on your shelf. You figure a shelf filled with 30 gallons of freeze-dried food is going to last your family months—it won't. If you were to stock only those gallons of food, you would need about 15 per person to last a month.

Ideally, you will want to stock a variety of freeze-dried foods, canned foods, grains and beans. This will give you the freedom to change up your diet and make balanced, typical meals. Although that might sound trivial when talking about a survival situation, maintaining a sense of normalcy is extremely important to your mindset. Your kids will appreciate sitting down to a normal meal of potatoes, spaghetti and a slice of bread. All of which are possible with a well-stocked food storage.

These are some key items you will want to include in your food storage.

Meats

- Tuna
- Spam
- Chicken
- Sardines
- Jerky
- Textured vegetable protein

Grains

- Flour

- Whole wheat
- Oats
- Cornmeal
- Rice

Vegetables

- Variety of dehydrated vegetables
- Canned veggies
- Freeze-dried vegetables
- Dehydrated potatoes sliced, shredded
- Instant potatoes

Fruits

- Dehydrated fruits
- Canned fruits
- Fruit leathers

Dried beans

- Pinto
- Kidney
- Navy
- Great northern

Dairy

- Powdered milk—best for cooking
- Instant milk—best for drinking
- Powdered butter
- Powdered cheese

Pasta

- Spaghetti noodles
- Macaroni noodles
- Egg noodles

Condiments

- Salt
- Sugar
- Honey
- Variety of spices i.e. onion powder, garlic salt, oregano, cilantro
- Bouillon for soups

Luxury Goods

- Chocolate
- Chocolate powder
- Coffee
- Alcohol

Renewable Food Sources

If you live in a rural area, it makes sense to raise your own animals for the purpose of survival. A renewable food source like chickens, pigs and even cows are one way you can ensure your family always has food to eat. Chickens are prolific breeders as are pigs and rabbits. Cows are a little tougher to manage and do not reproduce s often. Goats are a better option and can provide milk.

Along with raising animals with the purpose of using them as a food source, you will also want to experiment with gardening. Not everybody can be a natural green thumb. You will want to get the hang of it before you need it to survive. Creating a garden space now will give the soil time to become fertile and more pliable to your attempt to grow food.

Water

Water is by far the biggest space hog in your food storage plan. It is bulky and there is really not much you can do about it. You need to store 1 gallon of water for each person in the house per day. 4 people in the home multiplied by 30 days equates to 120 gallons of water. That is just for drinking. That isn't factoring in cleaning or bathing. Don't panic yet. We are going to discuss some ways you can store enough water for your family. On a side note, water is an absolute necessity. It is more important than food. You can't just hope it will rain enough to keep your family watered.

If you have a well, purchase a hand pump so you can continue to pump fresh water. You can store a little water and pump the rest as needed. If you live near a body of water, you can also rely on it to supply your family with the water it needs to survive. Although it may not sound possible, that old fish pond down the road is perfectly suitable for supplying your family with water. If you are going to be hauling water, make sure to do it when it is safe. Use the buddy system whenever possible. If you are not sure about the water in your area, buy a map and use a compass to create a circle with a 5-mile radius around your home. Walking 5 miles is not a lot of fun, but it can be done. Having a wagon or cart is always a good idea if you are planning to haul water.

All water is considered dirty, unless it is coming from a well and you are not dealing with some kind of biological warfare that contaminated your water. You will need to clean all water before drinking it. You will need to store some kind of water purification system in your bug in supplies. Tablets, water filters and water purification straws are all options. Boiling the water is also a possibility if you have a barbecue or camp stove available. One of the benefits of bugging in is the fact you will have your entire kitchen at your disposal.

A useful tip about boiling water for drinking: the second the water comes to a boil it is safe! There is no need to waste water by boiling it for 5 to 10 minutes. This causes steam and evaporation and your precious water is lost! Boiling the water for a certain amount of time is a myth. The very second the water reaches boiling temperature, the pathogens are effectively killed.

Cisterns

You can plan ahead by storing a large amount of water in large vessels often referred to as cisterns. You will need some space on your property to place the cistern. They are available in a variety of sizes with some as small as 50 gallons with large ones big enough to hold 1000 gallons. These are often used on farms and places where water is scarce. There are a couple of different options you can use to place the cistern. Bury it slightly uphill from the house to take advantage of gravity or place it in the backyard or if possible, on a hill. A pipe will feed water into the house using gravity. You could also use a hand pump to pump the water out of the vessel. It is a wise idea to have a rain catchment system that will feed the cistern. Rain water is generally considered safe to drink, but if you are dealing with nuclear fallout or biological warfare, it would need to be cleaned. To be safe, boil all water before using.

Pools and Hot Tubs

Your backyard pool or your neighbor's backyard pool if they have bugged out is an excellent source of water. An average in ground pool can hold around 17,000 gallons of water. That is certainly enough to last you a while. It will be chlorinated, but the water still needs to be cleaned before drinking. A benefit to using a pool is the open top will allow it to catch rainwater. An in ground pool is not your only option. Even the kids' kiddie pool will hold water. If it is full, you have a few gallons. Leave it uncovered to catch rainwater. If you have a hot tub on the back patio, you have about 300 gallons of water at your disposal.

Rain Barrels

These are an affordable way to store 50 gallons of water. Set your rain barrels outside at the corner of your home's roof to take advantage of the runoff from a rain storm. You will be amazed at how fast these barrels fill up after a single storm. You will want to cover the top with a screen to try and keep out the majority of the debris that will run off the roof of the house and into the barrel. Keep several barrels on hand. When one barrel gets full, quickly exchange it with a new one to save every drop of water possible.

You can buy ready-made rain barrels at your local hardware store for anywhere from $50 to $100 or you can make your own for under $10. Check with restaurants and container stores and ask to buy their 50-gallon food-grade barrels. NEVER buy a barrel that has previously held chemicals. Many places will give away these barrels or leave them outside for trash pickup. One man's trash is most definitely another man's treasure! Buy a spout at your local hardware store. Drill a small hole for the spout towards the bottom of the barrel and seal it with silicon. It is an easy project that could end up saving your family's life one day.

Bottled Water

Hundreds of bottles of water are often what preppers think of when it comes to planning their emergency bugging in supplies. Bottled water is certainly convenient, quick and easy, but it is also very expensive when you consider how many gallons you need per day. Not to mention, the amount of storage space it takes is pretty substantial.

You can buy the 5-gallon water bottles to be a little more cost effective. However, these still take up a lot of space. Ideally, you want to have a supply of bottled water, along with one of the above sources to replenish the water when it is gone.

If you are planning on bottling your own water to save money, this is a possibility, but there are a few things you need to know. Do NOT use old milk jugs to store your water. This is a messy disaster waiting to happen. The jugs are made of a thin plastic that will break down over time and not a long time. It could be as little as six months before your pantry is flooded by a milk jug cracking and leaking water everywhere.

These are some containers you can use to store water long term.

- 2-liter pop bottles
- Juice bottles
- Water bottles
- 5-gallon buckets with lids
- Store bought water vessels

Before you can put your water on the shelf in your emergency food storage, it needs to be treated if you are bottling it yourself. Most people will use bleach to treat the water. While this is effective and will keep the water clean and safe to drink without further treating, it will only keep the water safe to drink for up to six months. However, and this is a big one, if you are using water from your tap and your water is already treated (which most public water is) you do not technically need to add bleach before storing. This is one of those topics of debate among preppers. It is personal preference, but many decide to err on the side of caution because you just never know—unless you have tested your tap water to check the chlorine content.

You will need to add a drop of bleach to a gallon of water and about 5 to 10 drops to large 5-gallon containers. Bleach is safe to add to your water in these minute levels. It will keep bacteria and mold growth down as your water sits on a shelf. If you are going with treated water, date the containers so you can ensure they are always fresh and ready to go. If you have fallen behind on your rotation duties and a disaster happens, you can still use the water you have stored if it is out of date. You will simply need to boil it or use water purification tablets before drinking.

When you first open a bottle of water you have stored with bleach, be prepared to smell chlorine. Let the water sit in a bowl or in the bottle with the lid off for about 30 minutes to let it freshen up. Swirl the water to help air get to the water.

How to Store Your Dry Food

If you are storing dried food like beans, rice and other grains, you need to store it properly in order to keep it fresh and free of pests. Buying in bulk is often the best way to go when purchasing dry goods. They are typically sold in plastic bags. You don't want to store them like that if at all possible. It is better to store beans, rice and grains in 5-gallon food-grade buckets with snapping lids. This will help keep out rodents that will chew right through those plastic bags. You can help prevent other pests from destroying your food stores by adding a few bay leaves to the bottom of the bucket before adding your food.

Another option is to store food in Mylar bags. The bags are vacuum sealed and can be used repeatedly. They keep food fresh for years and when stored inside a plastic bucket, you can keep out unwanted pests as well. If you are storing pastas or flour products, you will want to put the items in the freezer for a week or so before putting it in your food storage. This will kill all the weevil eggs that are in these products and yes, they are a real thing. Leave flour sitting in a warm, dry area for a few weeks and then take a look. You are likely to find tiny little bugs crawling through it.

If you have purchased freeze-dried food, you have probably seen those fantastic shelf life dates on the can. Many boast the product in the can will last for up to 25 years when stored properly. Key words there are stored properly. Your food storage, especially in the aftermath of a major disaster, isn't going to exactly be ideal. To get those kinds of shelf lives, they are referring to the foods being stored in a cool, dry, dark area at a perfect 60 to 70 degrees and the cans are unopened. Now, if you have that place in your home today, by all means use it. That is the perfect storage place. If you don't have that place, than do your best to store your food in a pantry that is not in direct sunlight, is dry and will not reach temperatures above 80.

If you have the means and the space on your property, a root cellar is an excellent storage place for some of your fresh food items. Because you never know when disaster strikes, you will always want to keep a fresh crop of potatoes, apples, carrots and onions in your root cellar. Fresh fruit and veggies in survival situation are akin to manna from heaven. You can store these foods up to a year in a root cellar by following recommended tips and guidelines. You can also store canned foods in your root cellar. Just make sure you are always rotating your food to avoid it spoiling and going to waste.

Once you open one of those cans of freeze dried foods, you have about 30 days to eat it before it becomes stale. If you have a family of four, you can easily use through a can before it becomes stale. The cans come with lids that you will want to use to keep pests out in a survival situation. Remember, cockroaches can survive pretty much anything—including a nuclear bomb. Cockroaches, mice and other pests are going to be hungry too and your food supply is going to look mighty tasty.

You can still eat food that is past its "use by" date in most cases. It may not taste quite as good, but it is still edible if not a little crunchier than usual. The best if use by is simply a guideline and does not mean you have to toss everything out. In many cases, canned foods do not have use by dates on the can or label. You will need to use your best judgment about the condition of the food.

ALWAYS check your canned food before opening and eating. Botulism is a real possibility if cans have not been stored in optimum conditions. Botulism is fatal. Home-canned foods are especially susceptible to botulism and need to be carefully inspected as well. The following are a few signs that a can of food is not safe to eat—not even a little bit!

- Rust around the edges of the can
- Dented cans need to be carefully examined to determine if there is even the slightest perforation in the can
- Bulging cans—the lids are pushing up and out
- Leaking from a can
- Food inside is molded
- Liquid in the can is abnormally cloudy
- A foul order indicating spoilage

Medical Supplies

Bugging in allows you to stock a lot more medical supplies than bugging out. Although you probably don't plan on any major medical emergencies, you are going to be doing things you may not normally do in order to survive. Accidents are inevitable. You need to be prepared to treat a wound to prevent an infection from setting in. A small cut on your finger may not be a big deal today, but in a survival situation, it could mean life or death. You have the freedom to stock a little or a lot, but if you have the means; always go on the high side. All of your preps could one day be used as bartering tools.

- Boxes of band-aids
- Several rolls of gauze
- Medical tape
- Boxes of gauze pads in varying sizes
- ACE bandage
- Bottle of pain relievers

- Latex gloves
- Cold relief medicines
- Anti-nausea meds
- Anti-diarrhea meds
- Triple biotic ointment
- Rubbing alcohol
- Peroxide
- Burn cream
- Antihistamine—Benadryl
- Antacids
- Tweezers
- Emergency tooth filling kit
- Eye drops
- Calamine lotion
- Hand sanitizer
- Extra prescription meds if you can manage to keep an extra supply

If you are familiar with homeopathic meds, you will want to stock up on these items as well. If you have never experimented with natural medicine, it is a good idea to brush up on it. You never know how long a survival situation may extend and when over-the-counter and prescription medicines will be available once again. You need to have a backup plan.

Self-Defense and Security

This is a topic of debate for many. It is a personal decision each person needs to make. Having a gun to defend yourself and your family makes sense, but not everybody is okay with the idea of actually shooting another human. It is a legitimate argument. If you do choose to have a gun or several guns, you need to have ammunition. That is another area that can prove problematic. Gun owners who are preparing to rely on their weapons in a survival situation will need to make sure ammunition is stored in a sealed, climate controlled safe or ammunition can. Guns should be kept cleaned and in top working condition as well.

Pepper spray, knives and Tasers are all options as well, but hand-to-hand combat should be avoided at all costs. There is a strong possibility you will be injured in some way, even if you are the victor. Learning self-defense is a good idea and can help you ensure a victory if you are forced to defend yourself or your home.

The government recommends you keep a roll of sturdy plastic on hand to cover windows and doors in the event of a biological attack. You will likely have towels on hand to place under the doors as well. Vents will also need to be covered.

Miscellaneous Gear

If you are bugging in, you have the freedom to really load up on pretty much anything you need should you be forced to survive off what you have in the home. While food and water are typically the top two priorities, there are some other things you will need to survive a long period of time. It could take years for the world to recover from a major event. That means that although people will start to pick up the pieces of their lives and rebuild, there is still going to be a time period when grocery stores shelves are not stocked. Basic necessities are going to be in short supply, but in high demand.

If you have the room, you will want to start storing the following items as well.

- Toilet paper
- Feminine hygiene products
- Soap
- Heirloom seeds—these will produce fruits and vegetables with seeds that can be replanted to continue growing food.
- Hammer and nails—you never know when you need to make repairs
- Axe—chopping wood for heat will be a strong possibility
- Gardening tools i.e. shovel, rake, hoe—you are your own grocery store
- Hunting and fishing gear—see above
- Personal hygiene i.e. toothpaste, deodorant, shampoo, chapstick
- Face masks in case of pandemic or biological warfare. You also need to be prepared for the stench of death and decay.
- Heat source—wood stove, propane or kerosene heaters (have a supply of propane and kerosene on hand)

- Heavy duty garbage bags—there will not be garbage men and you need to keep your home clean to avoid bacteria and disease
- Entertainment—books, board games, crossword puzzles, cards are all things you can toss into your storage area that will help pass the time. You are probably going to be very surprised how much time is on your hand when you don't have computers, cell phones, gaming systems and television.
- Bleach—for cleaning your home and purifying your water. However, bleach does weaken over time. You can typically expect a gallon of bleach to last about a year.

Securing Your Home and Supplies

Creating an adequate food storage plan is extremely time-consuming and labor intensive. It can also be a huge investment of the family's funds. You need to protect it with everything you have. It is what is going to keep you alive when things are tough. If you are going to be bugging in, you need to make sure your supplies are secure and not susceptible to the looters and other folks who did not prepare. As was mentioned earlier, people are going to come looking. Many preppers are very secretive about what they have even among fellow preppers who they deem friends. This is because you just never know! People turn on each other when it comes down to a life and death situation. Put yourself in somebody else's shoes. If your child were starving, wouldn't you be willing to do almost anything to feed him or her?

It may sound a little cliché, but one of the first rules of prepping is not to talk about what you have. You can certainly talk with others about what they may want to store and what you think would be a really good idea to store, but you don't want to say, "I have a 12-month supply of food and water in my basement." Keep it to yourself! Educate your children as well. They don't need to tell all their friends about what they have in their basement. Kids talk and if they are starving after a catastrophe, they are going to tell others about what so and so told them a while ago. You would have a mob at your door and your family's safety would be in serious jeopardy.

Securing your supplies can be as simple as keeping them out of sight or as intricate as hiding them in a panic room or other secret space in your home. This is sometimes where people get the wrong idea about preppers. Preppers are often called weird or crazy for going to great lengths to hide their supplies. But, when you think of how much time and money is involved in creating a year's supply of food, it isn't all that crazy. People hide their valuables in wall safes and other nooks and crannies all the time. It is normal to want to protect things of value and when there are no grocery stores, government aid or fast food restaurants, food is going to be more valuable than precious jewels.

While a state-of-the art panic room is a dream many preppers have, it is just not feasible for most due to the cost. Bunkers are also a luxury that many preppers dream about, but again, it isn't always possible, especially for suburban preppers.

It is best to secure your home to keep out those who will try and take what you have. We will discuss securing your supplies next. A simple lock on a front door is not going to keep out the baddies. Windows and sliding glass doors are an open invitation. There are some preppers who have invested in bullet-proof glass for sliding glass doors. This is a great idea, but again, pretty costly. Many will go about putting shatter-proof glass in place of glass windows on the bottom floor of their houses. This is a common practice for people who are worried about burglaries. However, you need to consider the risks of living in a house that would impede escape if ever there were a fire.

Another way to secure your home's windows is by keeping some plywood on hand. When disaster strikes, or just before if you know it is coming, nail the wood over the windows to keep intruders from breaking the glass. If it is a storm system you are preparing to whether, this can keep your home intact as well and keep you safe from breaking glass.

Invest in sturdy door locks or create a bar system that makes it difficult to kick in a door. These can be found online or at some home improvement stores. Investing in solid metal doors is a worthy investment. DO NOT put pet doors in your front or back doors! This is an invitation for thieves in any situation. Bars on windows are an option, but you have to remember you are going to be living in your house when things are "normal." Bars on the window are often a signal that you have something of value inside and you may be targeted by thieves before disaster ever strikes.

Many experts agree that protecting your home's perimeter is the best way to go. It is likely the power will be out, but you can buy motion detector lights that are solar powered. This will at least give you advanced warning that somebody is headed your way. Cameras or a security system are great, but will only work if you have power. If you are savvy enough to hook your security system up to a car battery, that is always an option or maybe you have already invested in solar power.

You can still hide your food supply throughout your home or apartment. A single pantry may seem like a good place to store all your food and it is, but it is also the first place a looter is going to look. There are several other places in your home you could hide your food, water and other emergency supplies that will not attract the attention of unwanted visitors. Basically, you want to follow some of the guidelines mentioned in the hiding of a bug out bag. There are a few more places you can store food and other emergency supplies, including weapons. Check out some of these ideas and see if you can make them work for you.

- Behind the couch. You can create a behind-the-couch table that will successfully hide a great deal of food. There are can organizers that are as wide as the height of a can of food. You could stack several on top of each other and place between the wall and couch. Put a piece of wood over the top of the can holder and add a few pretty candles. It will look like a piece of furniture.

- Create a false bottom in your closets. Line up canned foods along the bottom of the closet. Put a piece of wood over the canned foods and dump your shoes, bags and what not on top. Anybody who pulls the closet open will see the typical contents.

- Your child's toy box is another great place to stash supplies. Create a false bottom that the kids cannot remove. Most kids won't bother trying to remove the bottom of a toy box anyways. Once they reach the bottom, they move on.

- You could certainly utilize the space under your bed, but realize many burglars and looters will look there first. However, use dark colored totes to stash your supplies in. Label the totes "winter clothes" or something along those lines. Thieves who are in a hurry may not take the time to rifle through the tote.

- Fill your attic space with totes and boxes of "grandma's things" and "holiday decorations," but in reality, your supplies would be mingled among the boxes of what would be perceived as junk.

- A hook on the back of your bedroom door that holds your bathrobe could double as a place to hide a weapon or a first aid kit. Hang the item on the hook and throw a dingy bathrobe over the top. Thieves won't look twice. Be careful not to hang anything too heavy as this may alert the thief to your hiding spot.

Teaching the Whole Family the Bug In Plan

If bugging in is your goal, you need to make sure the whole family is on board. You need to have a plan for each family member to follow in the event of an emergency. It is almost impossible to predict when or where disaster will strike. There is a good chance you and your family will not be home when it all hits the fan. If you are planning to bug in, you need to make sure you have a plan to get everybody home. Every family will have a different plan. However, every member of the household will have an ultimate goal of making it home. Check out the following example.

*You and your spouse both work. The spouse works outside of town, while you work in town. Your oldest child attends high school, which is within a block or two of your youngest child's elementary school. Plan A—you as the in-town spouse will figure out a way to drive, walk or bicycle to the kids' school. Oldest student will have already rounded up youngest sibling and will be waiting across the street from the school for in-town spouse to escort home. Out of town spouse goes directly home.

*Plan B-Oldest student finds younger sibling and makes the trek home along a designated, pre-planned route. In town spouse follows same route if possible to pick up the kids.

In the immediate hours and days following a disaster, your family may opt to hole up in the basement, a safe room or a designated area in the house. Typically, your best bet is below ground. If you have a basement, you will likely want to hide there until things have settled down a bit. You need each member of the family to know where they are supposed to be when they hear the emergency sirens outside or mom and dad have said, "This is it!" You, as the adult, will not have time to collect children, gather any additional supplies, lock up and get to the designated area. If you have several children, have an older one responsible for getting a younger one to the right place.

Plan ahead who is going to lock the front door, who is going to shut off the main gas to the home and who is going to get the pets into the home. Run drills often to make sure everybody knows exactly what they are supposed to do in an emergency. Teach your children the importance of dropping everything and getting into the safe room. You absolutely want everybody together so you can take a head count. If your home is already secured and you are planning on bugging in without holing up in a particular area, you still need a meeting point so you can account for every member of the household. This is also the time you will want to go through the checklist of things that needed to happen to ensure your bugging in is going to be a safe place for the family.

Bugging In Checklist
- Shut off all utilities just in case—water, gas, electric
- Lock doors and windows—put sticks in windows to prevent them from being opened
- Use wood to cover windows if possible from the inside so outsiders are not aware somebody took the time to secure the

home. The curtains or blinds will look normal hanging in the window.

- Make the toilet (see section below)
- Cover windows with blackout curtains or blankets if you don't have wood (you don't want others to know you are in the house)
- Grab flashlights and candles but only use when necessary to avoid detection
- Discuss what everybody will need to do for the next 24 hours
- Relax and keep everybody calm, sing songs, pray, read stories or do whatever helps your family relax.

Bug In Toilet

It isn't something anybody likes to talk about, but no matter what is happening in the world, humans still have to poop and pee. When you bug in, you are likely going to be in your home without a working toilet. If you live in the country and have a septic tank, you are still going to have to flush the toilet without power. This is a waste of water, but if water isn't a problem, consider yourself one of the fortunate ones. Because you are going to be in your home, you can't allow it to become filthy. Human waste harbors a host of bacteria and viruses that could make you and your family extremely ill. Cleanliness is extra important when you are bugging in.

1-Have a 5-gallon bucket ready
2-Have a roll of heavy-duty garbage bags

3-Line the bucket with garbage bag—to be extra careful, double line the bucket.

4-Use the bucket as a toilet and dump as needed.

5-When toilet isn't in use, cover with a lid to cut down on the smell.

If you are on a large piece of land and can safely go outside to use the toilet, do so. You can dig a hole in the ground, cut out the bottom of a bucket and place it over the hole to use as a toilet. Cover the hole every few days to cut down on smell. Place a rock or piece of wood over the area to keep animals from digging it up.

Pets—Do You Keep Them or Abandon Them?

Your family's pets are likely one of the family. You love them dearly and couldn't imagine leaving them outside as you bug in or leaving them behind if you bug out. That is a sentiment many pet owners share, but you must consider your family's needs first. Could you split the last can of beans with your pet? It isn't really fair to bring your pet along for the ride only to let it starve when food runs low. Sanitation could also be an issue if you are bugging in. If it is a cat, a litter box is adequate. If you have dogs, you are going to have to pay close attention to their bathroom needs. You will need to make sure you can open a door to let the pet out to do their business without calling attention to the fact you are holed up in your home. It is absolutely not sanitary to let the animals do their business in the place you will be eating and sleeping.

On the flip side of the argument, having what may be your best friend or your child's best friend by your side when things are scary is a huge comfort. This is true of bugging in or bugging out. Being able to pet your animal is comforting. Your children will take great pleasure in having a companion with them that is from their life before things got ugly.

There is also the possibility your pet could be an additional layer of security. You don't have to have an attack dog, but a dog will defend its owners and property instinctively. This is a handy tool to have along with you when you are trekking to a body of water to retrieve water for your house. If you have bugged out, a dog is a hyper-sensitive alert system. Dogs can hear and smell intruders and predators long before a human ever could. This is like an early warning system for you. It gives you time to hide or prepare for intruders.

If your dog has been trained to hunt, this is another very good reason to bring it along. There is a strong possibility you will need to return to the old ways of hunting and gathering. Having a dog along can make the job much easier and more effective. If you have bugged out and the temperatures are freezing, snuggling with your pet is an excellent way to maintain your core body temperature.

Once you have weighed all the pros and cons of keeping your pet or several pets with you, it is time to make a decision. You need to make the decision before an emergency arises. It is almost impossible to make a logical decision when your pet is yapping to come along with you when you bug out. It is an emotional decision that you want to take the time to evaluate carefully before you are forced to do so.

If you do plan on keeping the pets with you when you bug out or bug in, you need to expand your preps to include dog food. You will also need to factor in the additional water needed to support the animals.

Deciding to Bug In or Bug Out

This is one of the toughest decisions you will have to make. It is best to decide before an event happens. You want to use logic to make such a life-changing choice—not emotion. It is natural you would want to hunker down in your home, where all of your things are and where you feel most comfortable. Bugging in gives you the chance to really stockpile everything you need to survive in the aftermath of a devastating storm, an economic collapse or whatever it is that has befallen you.

There is always a lot of talk about bugging out, but that may not be what is right for you and your family. It does seem the prepping world gets a little bug out happy. People are always talking about the bug out bags and how to survive off the land. While that is all very important, why do that if you don't have to? Sleeping outside when it is snowing and the temperature is hovering around 20 degrees and you have nothing more than a space blanket to keep you warm isn't exactly ideal. Don't be too quick to plan on bugging out. It is exciting when you sit in your comfortable chair drinking your hot coffee and reading about it, but actually doing it is an entirely different ball game. Roughing it isn't always that fun once the novelty wears off. If you absolutely must leave your home, fine, but don't just assume you have to bug out when disaster strikes.

There are several factors that will need to be considered before making a decision. Do not wait to make such an important decision. Talk with your family members and get their input. If you know anybody who you would consider an experienced survivalist, get their opinion as well. Make a list of pros and cons. Brainstorm the various scenarios and make the decision to bug out if there is a terrorist attack but bug in if there is a pandemic or whatever the case may be. This preplanning will make things go much smoother when it is time to take action.

Even if you reach a decision to bug in or to bug out, you need to be prepared to do the opposite, just in case. If you have decided you are going to bug out, there is a chance it will not be safe for you to leave your home if the weather is bad or there are gunmen out there waiting to take you out. On the flipside, if you have decided to bug in and a major storm strikes and turns your home to rubble, you need to bug out. Always have a backup. Part of the prepping mentality is to prep for whatever disaster may strike. You are storing food, water and medical supplies because there is a chance things could go very bad and you are going to be forced to survive on your preps. There are no certainties in a chaotic world. You have only yourself and your closest friends and family members to count on.

Where You Live Matters

Your decision to bug in or bug out is going to weigh heavily on where you live. If you live in a rural area on a nice piece of land and the nearest neighbors are a ½ mile away, bugging in is completely doable and probably warranted. If you live in an apartment in the city, bugging out may be a better option. As a general rule of thumb, preppers will want to get out of Dodge so to speak when things are in chaos. More people, means more problems, like people trying to take what you have. Large cities become targets for attacks if it is a war or act of terror you are up against.

One of the first rules of survival is finding shelter. If your home no longer provides you with adequate shelter from the elements it is time to go. Maybe it was damaged by a natural disaster or the foundation has been compromised by an explosion. If the shelter isn't safe, it is absolutely crucial to bug out.

Another factor may be the location of your home. Floods are often a side effect of certain natural disasters. Homes that are too close to a body of water and are at risk of being flooded should be evacuated. Apartments in high rises are often targets for bombs if we are under a terror attack or there is civil unrest. Earthquakes may make the structure unsafe.

You can determine what kind of natural disasters your home is most likely to experience by checking some history. Answer the following questions to help you identify risks that could put a bug in plan in danger.

- Do you live in tornado alley?

- Do you live along a fault line?
- Do you live high up in the mountains where snowfall is excessive?
- Are you surrounded by desert?
- Do you live near a nuclear power plant?

These are all questions that will help you identify any potential dangers that could make your home a disaster waiting to happen. No matter how much you love your home and you love the things in your home, if it is in danger of being destroyed with you in it, you have to leave it all behind.

Do You Have Somewhere to Go

Probably one of the biggest factors in determining whether or not you bug out is if you have anywhere to go! Do you bug out and plan on living off the land until things settle down (which could be months or years) or do you hunker down where you at least have a roof over your head? Really prepared people will have a location to bug out too. The second location is where they will hunker down and ride out whatever disaster has shaken things up.

The second location will likely be a smaller home located in a rural area. A cabin in the woods, a bunker underground or a ranch house that looks like it has been abandoned all make excellent destinations. These second homes can be stocked with everything you need to survive. However, and this is a big one, can you get there?

- If you don't have a car, can you and your family walk to the second location?
- If you have a car, do you have gas to get there?
- Will the route to your destination be closed if there is a major disaster? Bridge crossings are not always reliable.
- Is your route through the heart of the city?
- Do you need 4WD to reach the location?

If you are planning to bug out to another location, it is important you plot out a Plan A, Plan B and if all else fails, a Plan C route. If you are leaving the city, expect there to be a LOT of traffic. Highways may be clogged and you could end up being stuck in a horrible traffic jam. A backup plan may not be the quickest route and may involve a series of back roads, but they are less likely to be jammed up. Finally, a plan when all else fails should be in place. This may mean walking, biking or taking a boat to your secondary location.

Closing Thoughts

Preparing to survive an event that will turn the world as we know it upside down isn't easy. There are a lot of different bases to cover. We have it pretty easy right now. When we need something, we run to the store and buy it, borrow it from a friend or ask our family to help us get it. We have become accustomed to relying on various charity organizations and the government to help those who have been devastated by a natural disaster or some other horrific event. If we see something illegal, we call the police and they take care of the bad guy. If we get a broken bone or our child has a high fever, we go to the doctor.

Life isn't so bad when you list out all those luxuries we have and they truly are luxuries. When all of that is taken away, it is just you and those you can call true friends. There won't be anybody to come to your rescue. Taking the time to plan what you need today can ultimately save your life down the road and the lives of your loved ones.

Some people attach the words paranoid or crazy to the prepping movement. Those people assume nothing bad will ever happen. Some of those same people will also say that if something terrible were to happen, it is best to die with the rest of the community. A prepper will say *that* is what is crazy. Why give up when there is always a chance? If there is a chance you could keep your child alive and even thriving in a new world, it sounds crazy *not* to try and do it.

It is your life and you must do what you feel is right for you and your family. Don't worry about those who call you crazy and a freak. It is probably best if you don't really advertise you are one of those who is preparing to survive. There will be some of those naysayers who do survive and they will remember their crazy neighbor or co-worker and come calling.

The most important thing is to have a plan. Any plan. If you have some sort of plan, you will be better prepared than 99% of the population. And that advantage could very well be the thing that saves you and your family. So start prepping, start early, and stick with it!

*****

The Prepper's Guide to Firearms

Introduction

Welcome, reader. You have chosen to arm yourself, a decision that is not to be made without some serious thought. A firearm is a complicated and dangerous tool in the hands of the unprepared, but to those that understand them and handle them carefully, a firearm is a valuable addition to your collection of skills and equipment. In any prepping or survival situation, having a firearm, and knowing how to use it, will very likely separate the people who survive and thrive from those who don't. You've made an important first step towards protecting yourself and your loved ones.

This guide will be focusing on pistols, as that will be the most likely choice for your average prepper or family. Of course, there are many other options out there, and if you are a more experienced marksman, you will certainly be able to branch out in your firearm selection. But for the ease of this guide and for the average family or preppers or survivalists, a pistol is going to meet each and every need that they have for a firearm.

For the beginner, this guide will teach you what you need to know so that you can use your firearm without being a danger to yourself and those around you. Once you have reached that level of basic competence, or if you are already familiar with firearms, this guide will go into some depth on training and use of firearms, so that you can continue building your skills.

You need to consider a variety of different factors before you choose your firearm, and you will have many tasks and responsibilities to handle once you finally have it. All of these responsibilities are yours, but you will have this guide to help you along the way. You will be led through the consideration, selection, and purchase of a firearm. You will also be introduced to safety, operation, and how to train and employ the weapon, so that you can use it effectively and safely.

Remember, however, that this is only a guide, and it cannot cover every situation. In the end, you are the one who is going to be making all the important decisions, from which firearm to choose to whether or not to use deadly force in a tense situation. Should you ever be put to the test, it is a brutally simple pass-or-fail, live-or-die evaluation. This guide will not be with you to help you through if and when it happens. It is up to you to train and study the concepts within, until you are fully proficient with your weapon. You have to put in the work.

That being said, let us begin.

Select a Pistol

Budget

Since you have decided to buy a pistol, you need to work out a budget. Not only do you need to set aside money for the weapon itself, but you also need to think of the long-term investment in ammunition and accessories. You will need to be able to buy ammo for regular practice, or you will not have the skill needed to use your pistol when it counts. No amount of quality equipment will make up for that lack of skill. Accessories and spare parts are another expense you have to include.

A good rule is that if you cannot afford the ammo, then you cannot afford that pistol. Consider that you will need to be setting aside ammo for later. After a collapse or a when you enter a survival situation, you will not be able to drive to the store and buy the rounds you need. You can only rely on what you already have, as scavenging will not be a reliable source for very long, if at all. A lot of the ammo out there is going to be in the possession of other people, and they are not likely to give it to you—unless you consider incoming fire to be a valid form of ammunition exchange. Make sure that you have plenty for your needs, and remember: the more, the better - no exceptions.

You should have several hundred rounds at minimum, and a few thousand is a much better idea. This might sound like a lot, but consider that over a quarter of a million rounds are fired for every insurgent killed in Iraq and Afghanistan. And that number is coming from highly trained soldiers. For the average Joe, it's going to be a higher ration still. A lot of that is training requirements, and automatic and suppressive fires burn through ammo much faster than semi-automatic pistol fire, but it does a good job of showing why you want plenty of ammo and plenty of practice. You can go through a full magazine in just a couple seconds with ease. Practice will reduce the number of rounds you need to fire to get the job done, but you will still want as much as you can get, and you will still need to buy the rounds with which you are training.

Magazines are usually relatively cheap, and you should get enough to last you for some time. Magazines will wear out and do not last as long as your pistol will, so you need replacements. The same goes for spare parts; some pieces wear out faster, or are more fragile in general. A broken firing pin, for example, means you now possess a paperweight instead of a pistol. A spare pin fixes all that, and lets you keep on going. While you could get a set of machinist's tools and all the necessary equipment to fabricate new parts, it is far more economical to simply buy them and store them away for the day you need them.

Accessories for your pistol are an additional expense that depends on your personal taste. You can get laser sights, lights, custom grips, laser grips, scopes or optics, and more. If you can think of it, you can probably buy it. The only one that you really need is a set of night sights so that you can still see the sights in dim light or darkness. Note that I am not talking about night vision, which will run you thousands of dollars, but basic glowing paint or tritium sights that give off enough light to allow you to align them even in low light conditions. You have plenty of other accessories from which to choose, but you might consider if another pistol already has the feature you want to add on before you spend the extra money on it.

As you can see, budgeting out a pistol is not as simple as it might appear. Until you have your allotment for your pistol, this should be the farthest you go in the guide. Once you have decided how much you can set aside, then it is time to start researching and shopping, not before. This will give you time to make decisions based on careful thought, not impulse and emotion.

Types of Pistols

After you have your budget set, you need to look at the different types of pistols available to you. The four main options are the autoloader, the revolver, the carbine pistol, and the muzzleloader. Within each category are a variety of different pistols that may or may not be similar to the others. Take the time to get a good idea of what is on offer. Not all autoloaders are the same, and the same goes for revolvers. Carbine pistols and muzzleloaders are fairly specific, and will not be as distinctive as the other types, but you can still find differences between them. Look at all of your options, and then make your choice. This is not a decision that you want to rush, so take your time and do your research before you buy.

Whichever you pick, be sure that it is best *for you.* Each pistol will have its own strengths and weaknesses, and will fulfill different roles. Do not allow yourself to be convinced to buy something that does not fit your needs because if it does not suit you, then it is not best *for you* even though it may be an excellent weapon in its own right. If you want something you will be able to conceal, look for a good concealed carry pistol. If you want to use it for hunting game, look for the best hunting pistol. If you are worried about the fighting and violence after a collapse, look for the best combat pistol. In the end, the pistol that does what you need it to do is the best pistol, no matter what it is.

Revolvers

Revolvers operate exactly as the name suggests. A rotating cylinder with multiple chambers holds a round in each chamber and cycles them to line up with the barrel as the action is cycled. Unlike the other two types of pistols, revolvers do not rely on the round being fired to cycle the action. The revolver is cocked by pulling the hammer to the rear, and when the trigger is pulled, the hammer swings forward to strike the primer and fire the round.

Revolvers have one of two types of actions; the single action has one method of operation of the action, double action has two. Single action revolvers need to be manually cocked each time you fire, as they lack any mechanism to automatically cock the action. Double action pistols will automatically cock the hammer as you pull the trigger, but require a much stronger pull to get the hammer into place. You can still manually cock a double action, which will relieve some of the heavy trigger weight.

When it comes to hunting with a pistol, revolvers are the type typically chosen. They can also be carried concealed as an everyday carry pistol. Military and law enforcement have both moved away from revolvers as combat and duty pistols, and no longer see service.

Hunting is best done with a long barreled, high caliber double action revolver. You want a large round to put down large game, and many of the larger pistols are chambered for multiple rounds, so you can practice with less expensive ammunition and use the more expensive rounds in the field. As revolvers have no moving parts on the top of the gun, you can mount a scope or some other sort of optic, which will let you take game at a respectable range, comparing favorably to shotguns. With the right pistol, you can hunt just about anything living in North America.

A revolver can also serve as a backup for a rifle or shotgun, especially if you are hunting in areas with predators such as bears, cougars, or alligators. A long gun is far more awkward than a pistol at close range, and a revolver will allow you to get more rounds off in an emergency. Many people living in rural areas carry a pistol at all times for the purpose of defense against the local wildlife. In case of attack, a revolver can be drawn, aimed, and fired faster than a rifle, and it saves weight and the effort of carrying a hunting rifle on you at all times.

Smaller revolvers work well as concealed carry weapons. The simple mechanism allows for a much smaller pistol to be built, with some small enough to fit in your hand. Hiding one of these on your person is as simple as could be, as you could fit one in your pants pocket if you wanted. It is hard to notice such a small item when you are intentionally trying to hide it.

In summary, revolvers have several advantages over other designs. They have a wide range of cartridges, meaning more options for loads on both ends of the spectrum, large and small. They are mechanically simple, and have fewer parts that can break, which also means that they are simpler to operate. It does not require nearly as much practice to load and fire as other types of pistols do. The all-metal construction makes it harder to damage them and they are not as susceptible to extreme heat and cold.

Revolvers do have their drawbacks. They are almost entirely made of metal, with the grip being the only part that uses any other materials, so they tend to be heavy for their size. They are more sensitive to obstructions, and need more attention when they are being serviced to prevent buildups of dirt, rust, or carbon that will affect the action. Without constant care, a revolver can easily seize up and become an expensive chunk of steel until you dismantle it and scour it clean. They are harder to shoot than other types of pistols, as they are both heavy in the hand and on the trigger. Trigger pull is an important component of accuracy, and revolver triggers are not very forgiving to the novice. They have by far the smallest capacity among firearms, with the typical cylinder holding a mere five to seven rounds.

Autoloaders

        Autoloaders are magazine fed, semi-automatic pistols that use gas pressure and recoil to cycle the action, extracting and ejecting the spent casing and feeding in a new round each time the weapon is fired. Magazines are inserted into the bottom of the handgrip/magazine well, and the slide is pulled to the rear and then sent forward to feed a round into the chamber. Autoloaders will be either hammer or striker fired, though there is little significant difference between the two designs. Hammer fired autoloaders have an external hammer with a double action, allowing it to be fired whether or not the hammer is cocked. After the first time the pistol is fired, the slide automatically recocks the hammer as it ejects the case. Striker fired autoloaders have a spring-loaded striker within the slide that is automatically cocked each time the action cycles.

        Hunting with an autoloader is rare because so few autoloaders are suited to the task. Autoloaders have many options for concealed carry, making them a popular choice. Military and law enforcement made the switch over to autoloaders decades ago, as they are a superior service or duty pistol.

        Using an autoloader for hunting is not advised. The inherent characteristics of these pistols make them unsuitable for hunting. Only a few autoloaders are chambered in a caliber suited for hunting, which drastically limits your choices. The moving slide makes mounting a scope problematic, reducing the range at which you can effectively target game. They are light, which makes the recoil difficult to manage on any reasonable hunting caliber.

The only situation in which you would use an autoloader for hunting is as a backup, in case of emergency. An autoloader should be chambered in a fairly powerful caliber, with larger calibers preferred, running hollow-points or other special ammo to do as much damage as possible, as fast as possible, at medium to close range. This setup can be used for hunting if needs must, but is really intended as a response to an attack. It is direct and brutal, and the goal is to put as many bullets into your attacker and hope that one of them gets something vital or it bleeds out before it can hurt you too badly. Using your pistol this way can be effective, but it is more of a last ditch resort than anything.

Concealed carry is a specialty of autoloaders. A variety of sizes are available to fit the owner. It is easier to fit a larger cartridge in a concealable autoloader, making the shots you have more powerful. They do not require as much material as the other designs, making autoloaders more concealable across the board.

If you want to conceal a pistol on your person, then you need to take into account your size. Shorter and slimmer people are going to have less space in which to hide a pistol. They will have to make sacrifices that a larger person will not. Autoloaders come in a wide variety of sizes to fit your particular needs. They are made as small as a few inches long, and they can still hold a respectable number of rounds in the magazine. An autoloader does not need to sacrifice as much from the caliber to save on size, so a small pistol is able to hold a larger caliber than the other types.

A larger caliber is going to require a larger pistol, but autoloaders can manage this much better than the other pistol categories. Concealing an autoloader is also made simpler by the narrow construction. Less material means less weight, as well, which makes carrying an autoloader a more pleasant prospect. Autoloaders pack more rounds and larger calibers into less space, making them a superior choice for concealed carry.

While law enforcement uses the autoloader as their main duty weapon, military personnel carry them as backups for their rifles. Both groups use them the same way; at close range or when they are riding in a vehicle. Autoloaders allow for quick follow up shots, and the larger magazines allow you to fire a lot of rounds very quickly. If you carry a rifle or a shotgun and it jams or runs out of ammunition at an inopportune time, having a sidearm can be a lifesaver. An autoloader will allow you to fend off an attacker until you can get your main weapon back in the fight, buying you some time until you can reload or perform corrective action.

Space is tight inside a vehicle, and longer weapons can be hard to handle and aim while you are still in your car or truck. An autoloader can easily be operated with one hand while you operate your vehicle with the other. If someone tries to carjack you, an autoloader can quickly be drawn and fired at your attacker inside the confines of your vehicle. They are also easy to store, as you can fit one just about anywhere in reach.

While autoloaders are more complex, they are very well engineered. This means that despite the fact that they have more moving parts than other pistols, they are still very reliable. The parts most prone to wear are easily available as spares, and autoloaders do not seize up as easily as other types of weapons, both among pistols as well as firearms in general. Not cleaning an autoloader is never a good idea, but it is less a problem than with many other weapons.

The advantages that autoloaders have are their size and speed. Being smaller than revolvers or carbine pistols makes them easier to carry with you, and faster to draw when you need it. Autoloaders can be fired in rapid succession, and they are easier to bring back on target because of their weight, which makes for more time to make accurate shots. There are easy to conceal, and do not suffer as many drawbacks from being designed for concealed carry.

The drawbacks of autoloaders are their lack of power and range. They have fewer of the large, powerful calibers available, and those that do often sacrifice much. Range is a problem because of the inability to attach a scope to an autoloader and the shorter distance between the sights. They are designed for close quarters work, and suffer when used beyond this.

Carbine Pistols

Carbine pistols are scaled back versions of a full sized carbines or rifles. They are based off of the semiautomatic civilian versions of military rifles such as the M16 or AK-47. The changes in the design involve removing the stock and shortening the barrel to more manageable proportions, although it varies on the weapon being modified. They use a variety of different actions, such as gas piston or gas impingement, depending on the rifle from which it is derived.

Carbine pistols are very useful for hunting. They use rifle ammunition, which has far more power and range than comparably sized pistol ammunition. Scopes and optics designed for the larger rifles will fit their smaller counterparts just as well, and the sights that come with carbine pistols are designed to be used out to five hundred meters or more. The calibers available are enough for most anything you are likely to come across.

You may have problems with large game as the calibers best suited to hunting them are not suitable loads for carbine pistols. If this is the case, then a carbine pistol should only be used at ranges where you can quickly fire several shots at your prey. Dangerous game is less likely to be a problem because of the magazine size and the fact that you are firing a rifle round. If twenty or thirty rounds cannot bring it down, very little else would have been able to, and you should not have been hunting it in the first place. Keep these limitations in mind if you plan to use a carbine pistol as you main hunting weapon.

A carbine pistol cannot be concealed short of a backpack or a messenger bag, so do not even try. If you need to infiltrate an area without looking like a threat, a carbine pistol can do the trick, as it is more concealable than a full sized rifle, while offering similar firepower. Tuck it in something subdued, and carry it right in. Other than that, it simply cannot be done; any attempt will fail, and will draw more attention to you than if you simply carried it openly.

Keep in mind that it will take longer to get to it, as it has to be put away, where you can carry other pistols on your body without anyone knowing.

Carbine pistols really shine when they are used as a combat weapon. They are maneuverable in close quarters while still being useful at a distance. Military personnel and bodyguards the world over use weapons very similar to carbine pistols, such as personal defense weapons or submachine guns. In fact, submachine guns have largely been replaced with short barreled rifles, which is basically the same as a carbine pistol with a stock attached*.

*Note that attaching a stock to your carbine pistol without the proper paperwork and permissions can be a very serious crime, and simply possessing a stock that can attach to a carbine pistol is considered the same as having it attached. Make sure that you are not breaking any laws.

If you are worried about heavy fighting then the carbine pistol is your best option. Realistically, a rifle would be best, but sometimes this is not available to you. If you live in an area that has banned you from owning a rifle, the carbine pistol is the next best thing, being almost a rifle itself. No other pistol is going to give you the same options and features all in one package as a carbine pistol does. As a hybrid of rifle and pistol, they are far and away the best option if you are going to face lawlessness and disorder.

The main advantage of carbine pistols is that they allow you to have nearly all of the benefits of a rifle while they are still legally considered to be pistols. They have better range and power than other pistols. They can mount all the accessories of their parent rifle, giving you plenty of options for customizing your weapon to you.

They are also useful for someone who needs a rifle but cannot handle the size and weight. They also hold the most ammunition, with a variety of high capacity magazines available beyond the standard twenty or thirty round magazines that come with it.

The disadvantages of carbine pistols are that they are still essentially rifles as far as functionality is concerned, even if they are a bit smaller. They are almost impossible to conceal, and cannot be drawn quickly if you need them while you are carrying concealed. They are many times heavier than other pistols, and you will have to carry it or sling it wherever you go, which can be tiring. They are not a sidearm like other pistols are, and should instead be considered a primary weapon on their own.

Muzzleloaders

Muzzleloaders are single shot pistols that are hand loaded from the muzzle rather than the breech. They use loose powder and a separate bullet instead of a single preloaded cartridge. The powder charge is added and then the bullet is pushed into place with the help of a ramrod. Once the bullet is seated, the muzzleloader is cocked by pulling the hammer back. Once it is fired, the entire process must be repeated to reload.

As they use black powder and bullets instead of a full cartridge, muzzleloaders cost very little to fire. Even in the case of a complete collapse, you will still be able to reload them, as you can easily make your own black powder and cast your own shot. Making black powder by hand is simple to do once you know the proper proportions, and the tools required are simple and easy to use, both for the powder and the shot. Supplying ammunition for muzzleloaders is a trivially easy task.

Muzzleloaders are excellent hunting pistols, as they were designed for that purpose. Concealed carry is not recommended because of the limitations inherent to muzzleloaders. The military abandoned muzzleloaders more than a century ago and they are no longer used in combat.

Muzzleloaders are useful for hunting all but small game. The large bullets do plenty of damage, and the accuracy of the pistols allow for precise shot placement. Mounting a scope will assist your aim at longer ranges, so that you can keep more distance between you and your prey. The accuracy is a necessity, though, as the long reloads will make it very unlikely that you will get a second shot.

If you are hunting dangerous game, muzzleloaders have one serious drawback. The single shot means that if whatever you are hunting decides to come after you, then you have just the one shot, maybe two if you can reload in time. If you miss, or only wound your target, you will not have much chance to make up for your error. The large bullets used in muzzleloaders will do plenty of damage, but it may not be enough to stop your prey with a single shot.

While it is possible to conceal a muzzleloader, this is not a use for which they are designed. With the large frame and carrying only one bullet, they are not suitable for concealed carry. If you do manage to conceal a muzzleloader then if you ever need to use it you will have one shot, then you will have to immediately retreat and begin reloading. This is a last resort, if you have nothing better.

Muzzleloaders are completely inappropriate for any sort of combat. While having one is better than being unarmed, it is not by much. Firing then having to hide for ten to twenty seconds or more to reload is a terrible tactic, and so any other type of firearm is a better choice. Retreat is preferable to an attack if you end up in a fight with only a muzzleloader. It is only in the most extreme circumstances that the muzzleloader should be used in a fight, and the situation is desperate indeed if you are forced to resort to using one. If you are at all worried about having to use your pistol for anything other than hunting, do not use a muzzleloader.

The largest advantage of a muzzleloader is that it is not legally considered a firearm, so you can buy one without having to register it or go through the background checks. In addition, both the pistol and ammunition cost less, especially considering the large caliber bullets used in most muzzleloaders. It makes an excellent hunting pistol, and provides an economical way to hunt large game.

The disadvantage of a muzzleloader is reloading. It takes a long time and is a complicated process. This means that firing multiple shots takes

Summary

Revolvers:
Pros:

-They have a wide range of calibers and more options for large calibers.

-They are mechanically simple with fewer moving parts.

-They can mount a scope.

-They retain shells after firing, leaving no presence and allowing for reloading.

-They are less expensive.

-They are concealable.

-They have a durable, all metal construction.

Cons:

-They are very heavy for their size.

-The trigger pull is heavy.

-They have low capacity and longer load times.

-They can be awkward and unwieldy

-They require frequent cleaning.

Autoloaders:

Pros:

-They are lightweight.

-They hold more rounds and changing magazines to reload is quick and simple.

-They are very reliable.

-They can be drawn and fired quickly

-They are concealable.

-They are easy to aim.

Cons:

  -They do not have many large caliber options available.

  -They are not accurate beyond close range.

  -They have wear issues with certain parts.

Carbine Pistols:

Pros:

  -They fire more powerful rifle rounds.

  -They are accurate out to longer ranges.

  -They have lots of options for scopes and accessories.

  -They are excellent weapons for a gunfight.

  -They have more options for large capacity magazines.

  -They have a variety of different types to match your needs.

  -They operate like the rifle from which they are derived,
letting you cross train.

Cons:

  -They are heavy.

  -They are expensive.

  -They keep any of the problems the original rifle had.

  -They are not concealable.

  -They can be difficult to control.

Muzzleloaders:

Pros:

-They fire large caliber rounds.

-They are mechanically simple with few moving parts.

-They can mount a scope

-They are accurate.

-They are less expensive.

-They use cheap ammunition.

Cons:

-They only fire one shot.

-They are slow to reload.

-They are heavy for their size.

-They are very loud.

-They need to be cleaned frequently.

As you can see, each pistol has its place, and what one pistol does well, another might not. It is all based on what works for you. If you are planning on bugging out and may have to fight your way out, a carbine pistol might be what you need. If you want to carry concealed so that you will always be prepared for an emergency, then an autoloader or a small revolver might be right for you. If you are going to be hunting or defending yourself from the local wildlife, then a large caliber revolver or a carbine pistol is where you should look. If you want a pistol for your wife or girlfriend so that she can defend herself, go for an autoloader.

Calibers:

Once you have decided on the type of pistol that you want, you need to consider the caliber that you want. The caliber should do what you need it to, whether that be hunting or defending your home. The number of calibers available is massive, and you can find one for almost any situation or purpose.

Calibers are designated by their approximate sizes of the bullets in inches or millimeters. .45 AUTO is an inch measurement, noting that the round in question is about .45 inches wide, specifically .452 inches. 9x19mm Parabellum is a metric measurement, which is actually 9.01 millimeters wide. The specific caliber is important, because each pistol is designed for one or more specific cartridges, and loading a cartridge other than what that pistol has been designed to fire is incredibly unsafe.

For hunting, you want a larger caliber, with more power. The .357 Magnum is about the smallest caliber that is acceptable for hunting, and will be sufficient for deer and similar sized prey. For large game, you would be better off looking into the .454 Casull or .45 Long Colt. These have the power and range to kill large game animals, including bears. You may want to look for nonleaded bullets in these rounds, as fragmentation can occur with faster rounds, and having small pieces of lead in your meat is not very appealing.

For a concealed carry, smaller rounds are typically better, as they take up less space. At close range, the lower power of these rounds is not a problem, and having more, smaller rounds is an advantage in a gunfight. Calibers like the .380 AUTO or the

9x19mm Parabellum are good choices, especially when using jacketed hollow-points. Larger calibers take up more space, and are more dangerous to be shooting in public because of the risk of over penetration.

Home defense and combat share many similarities, and so the same rounds will do for either of them. Pistol calibers should be enough to incapacitate or kill, such as 9x19 Parabellum or .45 AUTO. The idea should be to have a pistol with a lot of bullets, such as the 9x19, or a few very powerful bullets, like the .45. It comes down to a personal call to which style you prefer. If you require a rifle round, then either .223 Remington or .308 Winchester rounds are good. Smaller rounds allow you to carry more, but larger rounds do more damage and travel farther. Again, personal preference.

Whichever round you choose, it should be commonly available, or you will need to buy a lot of it. In the event of a collapse, you can no longer go to the store for ammunition, and finding a rare or specialty caliber on a scavenging run is not a sound plan. The alternative is reloading. Although it is expensive up front, you can end up saving a lot of money by reloading your own ammunition. The supplies are cheaper than the preloaded rounds you can buy in the stores, and if you can reload your own ammunition, you are in a good position. You will no longer be limited to the rounds you had before the collapse, as you can take the cases and load them again.

You should buy the cheapest ammo that will reliably feed for your training. Since you are going to be shooting it at the range and not at someone trying to kill you, it does not have to do anything but hit a paper target. For the rounds that you plan on using in a real life situation, you should buy quality ammunition. Jacketed hollow-points do much more damage than hollow-points do, so you are better off getting them, although they can be more expensive than full metal jacket. The exception to this is when you are planning on hunting large game, because you will need the increased penetration of a full metal jacketed bullet to reach deep enough inside the animal to do damage.

Comparison of Pistols to Rifles and Shotguns:

It is important that you understand how pistols are different from rifles or shotguns. Knowing what those differences mean to you in practical terms. Pistols come with certain advantages, but also have their disadvantages. You need to know when a pistol is or is not sufficient for the task at hand, or if another firearm is better suited to get it done.

Pistols are smaller, lighter, and faster than rifles and shotguns. They are also weaker and closer ranged. They can be concealed and drawn quickly and easily. Rifles are larger, longer, and heavier than pistols. They shoot larger, faster rounds, at longer ranges. They can only be concealed in pieces. Shotguns are larger, longer and heavier than pistols. They shoot larger shells, with different bullet loads.

Pistols are by far the smallest type of firearm. They are designed to be fired with one hand, and though the larger examples may need two hands to handle, they do not reach the size of either rifles or shotguns. They are not as heavy, and they take up less space. Rifles and shotguns are comparable in weight. They need two hands to fire because of their length and recoil. They are heavier and take up more space than pistols, shotguns even more so than rifles.

Pistols can be concealed on your person, ready to go. They can fit in a belt holster, in a jacket, or in a shoulder holster. When they are needed, it is a simple task to draw and fire them. Rifles can only be concealed if they are taken down into sections, and then only in a backpack, briefcase, or messenger bag. They have to be reassembled before they can be used, which will take a minute or two. Shotguns are not concealable, as they are simply too large.

Pistols use smaller rounds that do not have the energy of rifle rounds or shotgun shells. They can use high capacity magazines to carry more rounds, but the higher the number, the smaller the round, generally speaking. Rifles use larger, heavier rounds that travel faster and longer than pistols or shotguns. They also use high capacity rounds, but they do not have to sacrifice as much size for quantity. Both pistols and rifles have a limited selection of bullet loads, which are essentially limited to jacketed hollow-points and full metal jacket, as specialty bullets such as tracers are expensive and of limited utility to civilians, being designed to fit a military purpose.

Shotguns use larger shells, but carry few of them. They use a tubular magazine instead of the box magazine common to pistols and rifles, and so they have a restricted capacity. Shot and slugs are the two most common loads for shotgun shells, with the former being a collection of smaller pellets inside the shell, and the latter a single large bullet. The width of the bore allows for many variant loads for shotgun shells, with some examples including beanbags or flares, among others.

Drawing a pistol is much faster than a rifle or shotgun. They are so light that they can easily be pointed and aimed. The short eye relief makes matching the sights faster than those of a rifle, but a shotgun with a bead sight is almost as fast, though less precise. Rifles and shotguns are heavy and can be awkward to carry at the ready at all times. They are longer, so you have to fight your leverage to raise them. Finding your aim is slower because of the length of the eye relief.

Pistols have the shortest range due to the smaller bullets. The smaller powder charges in the cartridge and a short barrel limit the speed of the bullet, and the short eye relief makes aiming at long ranges a difficult task. Shotguns fall in the middle, as a rifled slug can be fired accurately out to over a hundred meters. Shot shells do not have nearly the range; the grouping of the pellets spreads out and slows down relatively quickly, but they are designed for closer shots, and can be improved with the use of a choke, Rifles have the longest range, as a long eye relief, long barrel, and large cartridge combine a more stable bullet, high velocity, and precise aiming to increase the range at which effective shots can be made.

In close quarters, pistols can be aimed and fired faster, but carry a weaker bullet. This can be compensated for by making follow on shots, taking advantage of the light recoil. Rifles and shotguns are more awkward up close, as the length can make it hard to bring them to bear if space is limited. Rifles are slower to aim, but the powerful rounds will often do more damage. Multiple shots are slightly harder to make, but not by much. Recoil is stronger than that of a pistol, but the weight of the rifle helps control it, somewhat. Shotguns do the most damage, as the shot and slugs it fires are both large and comparatively slow, and so they transfer more of their momentum to the target. Follow on shots are slower than pistols and rifles, but each shot inflicts severe injuries on the target.

Summary

Overall, rifles and shotguns are superior weapons, but a pistol is more versatile. Using a rifle or a shotgun for your main weapon is the best option, but if it not feasible, then a pistol is a good choice. A pistol can be carried anywhere you like without anyone being aware, and when you are up close, most of the problems either disappear or benefit you instead. Pistols are also easier to handle, which means that you can use a pistol where a rifle or shotgun would be too much. Women, children and the elderly can handle a pistol where they might struggle with a rifle or shotgun. Pistols are also good for introducing someone to firearms, as they use the same principles and fundamentals for their operation, opening them up to something larger later on.

Now that you know more about the different types of pistols, their benefits and their drawbacks, and you have considered your needs, you are ready to decide. Do your research, get other opinions, and find out what pistol you want. Make sure that you take your time and do this right. Once you have made the decision, you are ready to go shopping.

Purchase Your Pistol

You have a pistol in mind, and now you are ready to go buy it. You have a few different options when you look to purchase a firearm, and they have some very important differences. You need to understand what goes into the purchase of a firearm beyond the register. The options available to you are gun shops, Internet stores, auction sites, gun shows, and private party sales.

The gun store should be the simplest of them all, but because of the government requirements for firearms dealers, it is a more complicated process than it needs to be. Once you go in and select the weapon you want, they will give you a Firearms Transaction Record, or Form 4473, for you to fill out. You will need photo identification for them to check, and you will have to provide your information on the 4473. The dealer will take this and call up the National Instant Criminal Background Check System, or NICS, which is run by the FBI. He will give them your information so that they can run a background check on you and make sure that you are legally permitted to own firearms. None of this is applicable if you are buying a muzzleloader, as it is not considered to be a firearm under the law.

Once the background check is complete, and the dealer has verified that you may legally purchase a firearm, you may complete your transaction. This is usually a fairly quick process, and should not take more than ten or fifteen minutes. Sometimes the system gets backed up and it can take longer, but this is a rare occasion. If this does happen, expect quite a wait, as it can take hours or even days for them to work through the backlog.

If you choose to go through an online gun store or gun auction site, you will have to go through the same process. Since you have to complete the form and background check in person, you will have to have your pistol shipped to someone who holds a Federal Firearms License (FFL) so they can do the paperwork for you. This is usually the closest gun store, and they will probably have a FFL fee for you to pay for their time, which is in the twenty to thirty dollar range, plus the shipping fees from the seller. You can find some good deals online, especially on the auction sites, but you will have to pay a little bit extra to get it delivered to you.

Once you have passed the background check and paid, you can take your pistol and ammunition home. The sale is complete, and you can start to get familiar with your new firearm. However, the government now has a record of you buying a firearm. With the risk of registration leading to confiscation, this may be a concern for you. The government has used registration lists in the past to go back and find gun owners that did not turn them in.

If you do not want to leave a paper trail, you can look for a private seller online or at a gun show. Despite what you might have heard about the gun show loophole, it does not actually exist. You still have to fill out a 4473 and go through the NICS check if you buy from a FFL at a gun show. What a gun show does do, however, is make it much easier to find a private party willing to sell, and if you go through a private seller, no paperwork, no paper trail. You pay him, he gives you the gun, and you are done.

You can do this at his house, your house, at the gun show, or anywhere else you decide to meet. The gun show just happens to gather together a lot of men with guns into one place, that being the purpose of it. If some of the attendees want to buy or sell firearms, then that is their business. For this reason, if you are having a hard time finding a particular pistol you want, or you are trying to avoid leaving a trace, a gun show is a good place to look.

If you do decide to buy from a private party, or even if you buy used from a gun store, make sure to inspect the weapon before you buy it. You do not want to buy a pistol that has been neglected or abused, as it is more likely to fail on you. Check to see if it is clean or if it has signs of corrosion or other damage, and if it moves smoothly or if it feels stiff, loose, or shows signs of any other problems. If you have access to a range, ask if you can test fire it.

If you are buying from an individual, do not buy a firearm without having inspected and fired it. You can return a defective pistol to a gun store, but a private party sale is final. You might get lucky with someone being willing to take back a defective firearm, but you should not plan on it. Make sure that you are getting what you are paying for.

Once you have completed all the necessary steps, and you have bought your pistol, you must begin learning how to use it properly. Buying it was only the beginning. You have a lot to learn, and while it is a lot to take in, eventually it will become habit. The longer you work at it, and the more time you put in, the better your result.

Pistol Safety

One you have your pistol, firearms safety is the first and most important part of your training. Safety is something that you always need to have in mind, because one careless moment or small mistake can be fatal. Make sure that the pistol you bought to protect you and yours is not a danger, instead.

Good safety procedures are covered by the Weapons Safety Rules. You may not suffer a mishap each and every time you break one of the rules, but anytime an accident happens, it is because you broke one or more of them. If you follow them at all times, you do not have to worry.

First Weapon Safety Rule: Treat every weapon as if it were loaded.

Never act in any manner that you would not if your pistol was loaded. You never know when a supposedly unloaded pistol still has a round in it. Being unloaded is not an excuse. Any weapon that you handle should be treated carefully, loaded or not. Do not allow yourself to distinguish between how you treat a loaded weapon as opposed to one that is unloaded.

Breaking one of the other rules because your pistol is empty is a bad habit to learn. The reflexes and unconscious habits you pick up while you are handling your pistol do not care if it is unloaded or not. Violate safety while you have an unloaded weapon, and eventually you are going to do the same when it is loaded.

Second Weapon Safety Rule: Never point a weapon at anything you do not intend to shoot.

If you do not intend to shoot something, never point your pistol at it. You need to pay attention to where the muzzle of your pistol is pointing at all times, and it should always be in a safe direction. Point it at the ground or the sky, or point it downrange, and not anywhere else. Maintaining proper muzzle awareness at all times is very important. You should know where your pistol is pointed at any time, and check it often.

Third Weapon Safety Rule: Keep your weapon on safe until you are ready to fire

This rule may not apply to all pistols, as some do not have external safeties. If your pistol does have a safety, it should be engaged unless you are ready to squeeze the trigger. That means as soon as you stop firing, switch it back to safe. When you are carrying it around, when you put it away, and any other time that you are not actively shooting at something, you should put your pistol on safe. If you drop your pistol, the safety is another way to prevent an accident. If you have a safety, use it.

Fourth Weapon Safety Rule: Keep your finger straight and off the trigger until you intend to fire.

Never put your finger inside of the trigger guard until you are preparing to fire. If you are standing, walking, or running, you should have your trigger finger pointed towards the muzzle. This will prevent you from accidentally squeezing the trigger while you are not paying attention. If you become distracted and you place your finger on the trigger, you can pull it without meaning to, and cause a negligent discharge. It is best to get in the habit of laying your finger along the weapon and keeping it there.

If you have your finger on the trigger of your pistol when you are startled, fall, or are otherwise subject to sudden stress, your first instinct is to clench your fists, which will cause a negligent discharge. This is an involuntary reflex, and it happens without you having to think about it. The best way to avoid that reflex is to keep your finger safely out of the way until you need to squeeze the trigger.

Fifth Weapon Safety Rule: Know your target and what is behind it.

Every time that you squeeze the trigger, you should have positively identified your target as well as anything behind it. If you miss, you can send a bullet several hundred meters beyond your target before it finally stops moving. Anything that crosses its path will stop it, be that the ground, a wall, or an innocent bystander. Even if you hit your target, the bullet can penetrate through and continue on. Since the bullets are going to continue on until they hit something, make sure you know what that something is.

At close range, you may over penetrate your target, where the bullet keeps its momentum and goes through the target, continuing on until it hits someone or something else. This is extremely dangerous inside a house or in a crowd unless you are using certain types of rounds. In these situation, knowing what is behind your target becomes even more important.

These five rules form the basics of all safety practices. Commit them to memory, and never allow yourself to forget them. If you see those around you violating these rules, politely remind them to be safe, and likewise, accept any corrections they offer you. Do not become a danger to yourself and others because you could not be bothered to keep safe. Respect the weapon, and train safety so that you will train safely.

Pistol Operation and Maintenance

Function Check

Now that you have your pistol and are familiar with safety, it is time to learn how it works. Take it and look it over and find all the controls. Since each pistol is different, make sure to read your manual so that you know how yours works. Once you are confident that you understand how it works, you should perform a functions test.

Take your pistol and clear it. After you have properly cleared it, place the pistol on safe if it has one, and pull the trigger. If it is working, nothing should happen and the trigger should move very little, if at all. Take it off safe, and pull the trigger again. This time it should move freely, and you should notice some indication that it would have fired, as either the hammer should have fallen or the striker should have moved.

Now release the trigger, and without cocking or racking it again, pull the trigger. The pistol should not fire. Now cock or rack it and pull the trigger again, this time holding it to the rear instead of releasing it. The pistol should fire, then with the trigger still held down, cock or rack the pistol again. It should not fire as you finish cocking or racking it. Release the trigger, and then pull it again. This time it should fire. If all the checks pass, then the pistol is functioning properly and should be ready to be fired.

If any of these checks fails, stop what you are doing, and immediately put the pistol away. It needs to be serviced by a gunsmith, as the failure indicates that your pistol has a serious problem. Do not load or fire your pistol until after it has been checked and repaired. Any attempt to fire a malfunctioning pistol at this point is dangerous and irresponsible, and can result in injury or death.

Maintenance:

Cleaning your pistol on a regular basis is an essential practice for every shooter. It keeps the pistol operating smoothly and keeps it in good working order. Allowing your pistol to get dirty puts it at risk for malfunction or damage. It will also wear faster and is more likely to corrode than if you serviced it. The longer it goes without cleaning, the greater the issues, especially with revolvers and muzzleloaders, which will seize up if you let them get too dirty.

You need to clean your pistol every single time you finish shooting. If you set aside a certain amount of time to go shooting, some of that has to be weapons cleaning time. If you have the time to shoot, then you have the time to clean it afterwards. It does not take long, so take a rag, a brush, solvent, and oil to scrub it down, wipe it off, and protect it.

More detailed cleaning does not need to be done as often, but it has to be done regularly, whether or not you have shot recently. Once a month is a good schedule, and will keep any small problems that come up under control. You should also do a thorough cleaning after every hundred rounds that you have fired since the last cleaning.

Break down your pistol according to the instructions in the owner's manual. Scrub out everything. This is the time to get into all the cracks and crevices that you miss when you do a quick cleaning after a day at the range. Get out all the carbon and corrosion, clean all the pieces, and then give them a coating of oil to keep them safe from the elements. Put the pistol back together, wipe down the outside and give it another light coating, then put it away for next time.

The tools you need for cleaning are a brush, a bore snake or bore punch, rags or towels, cotton swabs, solvents, and lubricants. Brushes need stiff but flexible bristles, and are used to scrub off the pistol, inside and out. A bore punch is a set of rods with a cleaning attachment at the tip, and a bore snake is a long thin cord with a thick section at one end, and both are used to clean out the inside of the barrel. Use cotton swabs to get inside small holes or areas that the brush cannot reach, and to check for any residue after the cleaning. Solvents are used to break up carbon and corrosion, and the lubricant reduces wear from friction and protects the pistol from moisture and dust.

A simple cleaning kit can be assembled from common household items. Use an old toothbrush, a wire clothes hanger for the bore punch, old socks for rags, and cotton swabs and you have all the tools that you need for a thorough cleaning session. It is best to buy solvents and lubricants that are specifically designed for firearms, but you can get by with using mineral spirits as a solvent and motor oil as a lubricant. Be careful when you use alternate solvents, as they can strip the oil from the metal, making it more brittle and more vulnerable to corrosion. Apply a generous amount of lubricant if you do, to replace what was removed.

Pistol Marksmanship

Marksmanship is the skill and practice of handling a weapon so that you strike where you aim when you fire it. Besides safety, nothing will ever be as important as proper marksmanship is to shooting. You, as the shooter, have the most influence on the direction of your shots, but it requires skill to do.

Learning how to shoot well starts with basic marksmanship. The three components of basic marksmanship are breath control, trigger control, and sight use. They are easy to get wrong because they seem so simple. Nonetheless, they have to be done right. Learn them and practice them, and you will see improvement in your shooting and groups.

Breath control is the manipulation of your breathing to provide stability. It relies on the timing of your breath to take advantage of the stillness in between breaths. If you fire your pistol in the middle of a breath, your body will be moving. This will shift your aim over the course of the breath. To avoid throwing off your aim, you should during your natural respiratory pause, the short period of time in between the end of your exhale and before your next inhalation.

In order to understand the natural respiratory pause, you will perform a short exercise to demonstrate. Close your eyes and breathe in and out a few times, then take a deep breath and hold it for a count of four, then release it over a count of four. Once you exhale, wait a few moments until you need to breathe again. That break is the natural respiratory pause. While you are doing this, focus on the movement of your body. Feel the sight movement during breathing, and the stillness and relaxation during the pause.

When you breathe in and out, your entire body moves, although you do not notice it. All that movement will be transferred to your pistol, making it hard to aim. Your muscles also tense up while you are breathing, which makes aiming more difficult. If you fire when you are tensed up, you will reflexively relax at the very moment that you fire. When this happens, it is at the worst possible time, as you have no time to recover. Firing during the natural respiratory pause allows you to fire without the tightness interfering with your aim, and without the relaxation throwing off the shot at the last instant. Waiting until the pause removes all the interference is the best time to take a shot.

Trigger control is the proper operation of the trigger during a shot. If you do not move the trigger properly, it will interfere with your aim, and cause you to anticipate the shot. You must squeeze the trigger instead of pulling it to control the movement.

If you pull the trigger, you are exerting force in another direction from your aim. Your hand tightens when you pull the trigger, and it will shift your grip, and your pistol with it. This will pull your sights off the target, and force you to move them back. If you muscle the pistol back into place, you will be fighting yourself.

You will tire your muscles faster, and your aim will become unsteady.

Squeezing the trigger instead of pulling it stabilizes your hand and does not move any muscles besides the ones controlling your trigger finger. It moves the trigger directly backwards, providing a smoother movement. It is a more controlled movement, as well.

To demonstrate the difference, put your arm out in front of you. Make a fist with all but your index finger, so that you are pointing directly ahead. Pull your finger into the fist, and watch how your hand and arm move, muscles shift from your hand to your shoulder, and your fist moves. Next, return to pointing straight ahead, and squeeze your finger backwards like you are pinching something between your index finger and your thumb. Watch how little movement occurs in your hand and arm, and how smooth the movement is.

When you squeeze the trigger, it allows the shot to surprise you. If you expect the shot, then you will brace yourself for the noise and the recoil, even if you do not realize it. Instead, slowly squeeze the trigger to take up the slack, and keep moving until you fire the shot. That way you will not anticipate the shot, and that will prevent you from flinching or hesitating just as you fire.

Sight use consists of sight alignment and sight picture. Sight alignment is simply aligning the sights so that you have the pistol pointed in the proper direction. Sight picture is the proper focus and placement of the sights on target. Together, they will give you the correct aim. If you have one wrong, the other will likely be wrong as well, and this will throw off your aim.

When you aim down the sights, the front and real sights need to be aligned with each other. Looking at the sights while they are out of alignment is no good, as the point of aim will be incorrect. The method of alignment is dependent on the type of sights mounted on your pistol. The two most common are notch sights and aperture sights. Notch sights are aligned by placing the front sight post in between the rear sight notches, with the tops of both the front and rear sights level. Aperture sights are aligned by centering the front sight post in the rear aperture, both vertically and horizontally.

In order to demonstrate how sight alignment works, put both of your hands in front of your face, one in front of the other, and make fists with the thumbs up. Align the thumbs in front of your eyes, so that they make a straight line to a specific point. Now move the hand closest to you in any direction, taking it out of alignment. Keep your front hand in front of the aiming point, then move your head until your thumbs are aligned once more, and look at what you are pointing now. The distance between the two points is much farther than you moved your thumb, just as your point of aim and point of impact will be different if even a small misalignment of the sights happens.

Sight picture is the image that you see when you are aiming down your sights once they are aligned. The front sight post should be centered on your target. If you are firing at a circular target, you should be able to see a half circle above the front sight post. If you are firing at a silhouette target or a human, you should see the shoulders and head of your target above the front sight post.

When you aim, you should be focusing on the tip of your front sight post. Look at your target long enough to identify it, then shift your focus back to your front sight. Both the rear sight and the target should be blurred when you fire. It sounds counterintuitive, but if you focus on your target, you will end up striking around it. By focusing on the front sight post, you can ensure that your sights are still properly aligned when you fire.

As you can see, the differences between the right way and the wrong way to shoot is very small, and it is easy to do it wrong. The best way to shoot well is to focus on the basics. With practice and experience, you will learn to tell the difference, and you will be able to tell what your mistakes were after you are done. The simplest parts of shooting are the most important, and once you can do them right, you will see great improvement.

Ballistics:

An understanding of ballistics is a necessary part of training marksmanship. Ballistics is the study of the way bullets act once they have been fired. You will be introduced to the three stages of ballistics: internal, external, and terminal. Internal ballistics is the behavior of the bullet while it is still inside the barrel. External ballistics is the behavior of the bullet while it travels through space. Terminal ballistics is the behavior of the bullet once it strikes its target, until it stops all movement.

Internal ballistics processes begin as soon as the primer is struck and the powder ignites. When that happens, the expanding gasses begin to push the bullet down the barrel. At the same time, the heat from the burning powder causes the bullet to expand slightly, which helps it engage the rifling on the inside of the barrel. Rifling is a spiraling pattern inside the barrel that causes the bullet to spin, stabilizing it when it exits the barrel, and increasing accuracy.

Any obstructions or imperfections in the barrel will degrade accuracy, even if they are minor. One example of this is carbon buildup inside the barrel. Deposits of the burning gasses that push the bullet down the barrel will begin to coat the barrel. Over time, these deposits will grow larger and become more of a problem. Regular cleaning helps get rid of them, which will restore the accuracy of your pistol.

This portion of ballistics ends fairly quickly, but it is where the bullet gets its direction and momentum, which it will carry through its path until it hits something. This is why it is important that you hold your pistol as steady as possible while you are shooting. Any shifts in the pistol will transfer over to the bullet, which will alter the trajectory. You want to have as little movement as possible until the bullet has left the barrel.

As the bullet leaves the barrel, the external ballistics phase begins, and a separate set of ballistic processes start to influence it. The first is the release of gas as the bullet clears the muzzle. The escaping gasses vent out, but they do not do so evenly, so the bullet is slightly destabilized and begins a slight wobble. As it continues on, the spin imparted to it by the rifling will stabilize it somewhat, but it will also be affected by atmospherics like air pressure and wind, as well as gravity.

The bullet will want to continue on in a straight line, but gravity and friction will slow it down and bring it down. At long ranges, this can be quite significant, but it is negligible until you get out past a hundred meters or so. Past that, the resistance of the air will slow your bullet down and it will fall faster and faster. Longer ranged shots will spend more time travelling through the air, and you will have to include more of these factors into your aim.

Most of the different forces that alter the path of your bullet will not have as great an effect on it if you are going to be shooting in close. Even at the longer ranges that you can reach with a pistol, you will probably only ever have to deal with gravity, friction, and wind.

Once the bullet strikes an object, it begins the terminal phase of ballistics. The behavior of the bullet is dependent on the material it struck. A bullet striking a body acts differently than one striking stone, metal, or wood. This is important to know, as bullets will still retain some of their energy and momentum after the initial impact, and will act in predictable ways depending on what was hit.

When a bullet enters the body, it creates a wound channel behind it, which is called cavitation. The channel caused by cavitation will initially be wider than the bullet, as flesh is pushed outward by the shockwave of the bullet passing, but it will attempt to return to its original shape soon after, leaving a small hole. If the bullet passes all of the way through, the exit would will be considerably larger due to the shockwave pushing ahead of it. Inside the body, flesh can compress and move out of the way, but upon exit, no more space is available, and the shockwave will push it outward, leaving a gaping hole.

Another effect of the shockwave is hydrostatic shock. The impact of the bullet is transferred through the body, possibly damaging the internal organs. It can cause brain hemorrhaging and organ damage, even in areas of the body distant from the path of the bullet. The effect is more pronounced if repeated shots are made quickly. If multiple bullets strike the target, it can cause a sudden disruption to blood pressure, which can result in temporary unconsciousness.

Some rounds will fragment when they hit their target, sending several smaller pieces of the bullet through the body. This will increase the chances of a wound channel causing fatal damage. Fragmentation usually occurs in higher velocity bullets, or in jacketed hollow-point rounds. This is a definite advantage if you are trying to put down whatever you are shooting at, but it can be a disadvantage if you are hunting, as you would end up with tiny pieces of lead through the area where it was shot.

If a bullet only strikes flesh, it will travel in a fairly straight path until all of its energy is spent or it penetrates through. If it hits bone, the reaction is unpredictable. Sometimes the bullet will split into pieces and spread out through the body. Some of these pieces will follow the bone, which can lead them into areas of the body that are distant from the point of impact, doing further damage. Other times, the bullet will strike the bone and shed all of its momentum, which may result in the bullet being lodged inside the bone. If a bullet goes through a bone and continues on, it may begin to tumble, which will increase the size of the wound cavity. A bone that has been broken by a bullet is dangerous, as blood loss is usually quite severe and shards of bone often spread out from the impact site to do further damage to the flesh surrounding it.

When a bullet hits something hard like stone, metal, and some woods, it will deflect if it does not have enough energy to go through. When a bullet strikes at an angle, it is much more likely to deflect than to penetrate, and thin objects will stop a bullet from penetrating. The direction it takes from there is erratic, but the bullet will often follow along the surface. If it is a wall or some other long, flat surface, the bullet may skip along the wall. This is very dangerous to anyone along the wall.

If the bullet has enough energy to penetrate, it will continue moving, but it may still experience some deflection. Instead of continuing in a straight line, it will go in the same general direction, but it is not predictable once the bullet hits. The same effect happens when shooting through glass. In addition, bullets can penetrate farther through solid objects than expected. Common handgun bullets can penetrate a quarter of an inch of steel, and rifle bullets even more. Concrete, stone, wood, and other materials can be penetrated even deeper than metal. Walls, cars, and even small trees will not stop a direct hit from many pistols and most rifles.

Sight Zero:

You will need to zero your pistol before you start shooting and after each time you take your pistol apart to clean it. Check your owner's manual for instructions on how to adjust the sights on your pistol, so that you get the correct procedures for your specific pistol. Once you know what you have to do and have the tools required, it is time for the shooting portion of the zeroing.

You will need: three targets; two magazines loaded with ten rounds each for autoloaders and carbine pistols, or twenty rounds for revolvers and muzzleloaders; a support for your pistol, such as a pillow or seat cushion; a marker; ear and eye protection. A data book is an optional item, but it is good to have so that you can record your shots and make notes of any successes or mistakes.

Set up the targets side by side at twenty-five meters, with a few inches between them. Lay down the cushion at the firing line and get down in the prone position. Once you are laying on the ground, load your pistol with the first magazine or with five rounds, and get in as stable a stance as you can. You can use the cushion to steady your hands while you shoot, so that you can concentrate on aiming. Make sure to focus on your marksmanship fundamentals as you shoot.

Fire five shots at the center of the target on the left. Aim at the same spot each time you fire, until you have fired five rounds. Stand up, making sure to be careful with your pistol and mindful of where it is pointed as you do, and approach your target. You should see all five rounds in a group somewhere on the paper. Adjust your sights so that you can bring your next group closer to the center of the target.

Return back to the firing line and repeat the process, firing the next five rounds at the right target. Go and check, and adjust your sights again, so that you are closer to the center. If you were already on center, do not adjust your sights. Return to the firing line, and this time, fire the ten remaining rounds at the center target. From there, you should have all the shot data you need to make any final adjustments to your sights, and you should have a properly zeroed pistol.

If you have trouble shooting a group, then you are not ready for the drills. Keep practicing, keep reading, and keep shooting until you can group regularly. If you are at a range or know someone who is a good shot, ask him to help you. You have to be able to shoot properly before you can start learning anything else, or you will just end up wasting your time and money. Without accuracy, the skills you practice will be of no use.

Sometimes, the problem lies in your pistol and not your ability. Having someone you know is a good shot fire your pistol is a good way to locate the problem. If someone who shoots well has trouble keeping his shots tight, you may just have a bad pistol that needs to be fixed. The parts could be loose, or you might have some unnoticed damage.

Physiology of Shooting

When you shoot someone, your goal is not to kill them. Your goal is to disable him, in order to prevent him from doing you any harm. If you shoot someone, and inflict a fatal injury, he may still have enough time before he dies to injure or kill you in return. In contrast, a crippling injury to your target may not kill him, but it will prevent him from continuing to attack you. As such, you must always choose your shots for the best chance to disable your targets.

The reason behind the distinction is the ability of the human body to minimize and survive an injury. Aside from a durability and adaptability that will keep a man in a fight longer than you might expect, even injuries that will be fatal can be kept under control by the body. This is done through a set of physical and chemical systems in the body. They interact to numb pain, slow blood loss, and minimize the damage inflicted to the body.

A shot to the heart is a fatal wound, and only immediate surgical intervention will prevent death. That being understood, the heart can continue to beat for minutes afterwards, and the target can be alert and mobile for over a minute. Even if the heart suffers so much damage that is ceases to beat, the rest of the body can continue to function for several seconds, which is a long time in a fight for your life.

Skin and muscle are very elastic, and will stretch when shot. The cavitation of a bullet will cause a large disruption, but the body will return to normal almost instantly, leaving a wound smaller than the size of the actual bullet. The blood vessels become constricted, which limits the amount flowing through them if they are cut open. A wound that would cause massive bleeding can be slowed down to a trickle, and the permanent injury is minimized, so that time and energy spent healing is reduced.

The only way to reliably remove someone from a fight is to target the areas of the body that will prevent them from moving or acting. The best places to aim for are the central nervous system and the pelvic girdle. Either one of these will cause damage that cannot be ignored. Massive trauma is not optimal, but if enough damage is done it will suffice. Blood loss is the least effective, as it often takes minutes to bleed out, making incapacitation an uncertain prospect.

The central nervous system is made up of the brain and the spinal column. It connects to the peripheral nervous system, which is the network of nerves that reach every muscle, bone, and organ. All instructions for the body, from blinking to sprinting, start off in the brain. The spinal column transmits them to the nerves, which communicates between the body and the brain. Any damage to the central nervous system will disrupt the vital link between the brain and the rest of the body, and will likely result in death.

The best and most effective area of the central nervous system to shoot is the medulla oblongata. The medulla oblongata is responsible for the autonomic functions, or processes that do not require conscious thought. It is also the link between the rest of the brain and the spinal column No matter what you do, the instructions have to pass through the medulla oblongata. These include breathing, the beating of your heart, and, most importantly, your reflexes.

A shot to the medulla oblongata will instantly kill the target. As soon as the bullet penetrates it, the body will go completely limp and collapse. No reflexes will trigger, and all movement and brain function will cease, immediately. The medulla oblongata is the most basic level of the brain, and without its instructions and processes, nothing else can function.

Targeting the rest of the brain or the spinal column is also effective, as it does not require much damage to cause incapacitation. Once the rest of the body stops receiving instructions from the body, the target will be unable to harm you. An injury to the spinal column will incapacitate anything below the wounded area, and nothing can overcome that. Injury to the brain is even more serious, and is almost always fatal. Even if your target survives, he is likely to be knocked out by the impact.

The problem with targeting the central nervous system is its size. The brain and spine are small compared to the rest of the body, and are hard to hit on a moving target. The first instinct is to duck and lower the head, so you will have an even smaller target, and if you hit the head at an angle, then the skull can deflect the shot. The spine is also a hard target, as it is long and narrow, and surrounded by muscle and bone designed to protect the nerves within.

The pelvic girdle is a set of bones that together form the pelvis. They connect the legs to the rest of the skeleton and the muscles that connect to it support the body when it is upright and mobile. Several large blood vessels pass through the pelvic cavity, and it contains the bowels and reproductive organs.

A shot to the pelvic girdle will result in a loss of mobility in your target. Without the rigid support of the unbroken pelvis, the muscles cannot support the weight of the upper body and will collapse. The broken bones can damage the blood vessels, and the bullet may tumble around the area after it hits the bone, doing even more damage. With the target collapsed, it is simple to follow up with shots to the central nervous system to finish him.

If you do not kill the target immediately after shooting him in the pelvis, the wounds will likely prove fatal, regardless. Blood loss is likely to be a concern, as well as infection caused by any injury that ruptures the bowels. The pelvis takes months to heal even if the wounds are survivable, so the target is not likely to threaten you again.

The pelvis is a large target, and is easy to shoot. It is fragile, so damaging it is not difficult, and any shots that strike the pelvis can easily do more damage to the surrounding tissues. However, it is not immediately fatal, and the target may recover enough to continue shooting at you. It is most useful in order to stop someone charging you, as they will collapse and will only be able to drag themselves if they have to move.

Sensory

When you get into a fight for your life, your body is flooded with several chemicals that prepare you for violence. In addition to the physical effects mentioned earlier, you may experience unusual changes to your perception. These usually involve distortions or interference of vision, hearing, and fine motor skills, although others exist.

One of the more common phenomena is called tachypsychia, which means speed of the mind. This is believed to be related to the chemicals that are released in the brain during and after a fight. It is a perception that time is either moving very slowly or very quickly. If it happens to you, you will notice that everything seems to be moving slowly, including yourself, but that you have more time to react mentally to whatever is going on.

The sensations are temporary, and will end once the fight does. However, the body undergoes a corresponding collapse after a fight, which results in physical and emotional fatigue, leaving you vulnerable. This is especially dangerous to you if the fight drew the attention of others in the area, as you will be an easy target in the state of exhaustion. Whenever you experience a threat, whether or not you actually had to fight, be careful about relaxing until you are sure you are safe.

Psychology of Shooting

Most people panic when confronted by violence. Any sort of threat will terrify them, and they will not be able to respond beyond fleeing the area or, even worse, just holding still, shocked into immobility. A few do not respond the same way, and are in some ways drawn to violence. By learning what happens to both groups, you can train yourself to remain calm and focused even when everyone else has lost control.

Other people do not shrink from violence. The kind of person that does not hesitate to kill to get what they want is a predator. They can tell whether or not you are prey by the way you stand, the way you move, the way you act, and the way you look. If you want to avoid the attention of a predator, you must stop acting like their prey. Learn the ways of the predator and they will avoid you.

This is important, because if you have decided that you want a pistol with which to defend yourself, you have to prepare for the fact that you may have to kill another person. If you are not willing and able to do that, then all you will be doing is arming the first person you come across that is. Without the willingness to kill, your pistol is more a danger to you than to those that would do you harm.

Few people are comfortable with killing another person. This is a reluctance that is wired deep into the brain, so that people do not go around killing each other. The few that do not have this block, or in whom it is lessened, are not obvious. Until the time comes, you cannot tell whether or not you have the block or not, and by that time, it may be too late. Training yourself to handle a fight is a better plan.

The training you need to ready yourself for a confrontation is mainly psychological. Using your pistol is more than simply pulling the trigger. It is a decision to kill another person, and that is not a decision that is made lightly. You are responsible for making that decision, and the consequences of it. It is better that you make the decision ahead of time, rather than when you are faced with a life or death situation. Once you have decided and trained for it, you can evaluate each situation as it comes up.

Visualization and desensitization, are conditioning methods used to teach military and law enforcement how to react to combat, and you will use them as well. You do not have to train to the extent that they do, but the principles are the same, whether you are training for elite special operations, police work, or simple self-defense. It is all mental preparation for when the time comes to make the choice: fight, or die?

Visualization is a simple habit, and is very easy to add into your training. Simply put, it is imagining a situation, then deciding how you will react to that situation. When you step up to the firing line at the range, picture a scenario where you would have to shoot to kill. Go through the event in your head while you are shooting your course of fire, and it will build a response. If that ever happens, you will have a record of what to do.

The point of visualization is to create a memory. If you practice anything for long enough, you will eventually ingrain it into your unconscious memory. This is muscle memory, but it is actually a function of the brain, and not the muscles. You are training your mind to react a threat in a certain way, even though you have no actual experience. The visualizations will provide a workaround.

In order to overcome the block against violence, you need to desensitize yourself to it. Using the same principles as overcoming other extreme fears, you introduce it in smaller measures, then increase it over time. As you add more and more realism in your training, you will become accustomed to it, and it will not bother you in a real fight. Just like training to shoot, the more you train for combat, the more familiar you will be, and the less likely you are to panic like so many others do.

To begin, you should be using targets shaped like a human silhouette instead of the circular targets that are usually used. Eventually, you can move on to targets with printed images, and other even more realistic training aids. These will get you used to firing at real people, so that you do not freeze up when the time comes.

Mentally preparing yourself for a time when violence is your only option is just as important as training to shoot. Just as you cannot hit a target if you cannot aim, you cannot shoot if you cannot overcome your fear. Some fear is a normal thing, and it is can be used to keep you aware and alive, but it must not rule you. You can control your fear, overcome your reluctance, and fight for your life.

Courses of Fire

The following courses of fire are training drills to teach you simple shooting skills. These are the skills that you are most likely to need in a self-defense situation. Practice them as often as you can, so that you learn to shoot quickly and accurately.

You will be making four types of shots: single shots, rapid shots, controlled pairs, and hammer pairs. Single shots are made one at a time, with a chance to put the pistol down and rest your arms before the next shot. Rapid shots are made in sequence, reacquiring the target after each shot. Controlled pairs are two shots made in quick succession, aiming before each shot. Hammer pairs are two shots made almost instantly, aiming only before the first shot and keeping the pistol as steady as possible for the second.

Course of Fire #1: 25 Meter, Untimed

    20 rounds, single shots from the 25-meter line.

    20 rounds, controlled pairs from the 25-meter line.

This is work on basic marksmanship. Aim before each shot and remember the basics.

Course of Fire #2: 20-10 Meters, Untimed

    10 rounds, controlled pairs from the 20-meter line.

    10 rounds, controlled pairs from the 15-meter line.

    10 rounds, hammer pairs from the 10-meter line

This is work on closer targets. Remember that speed is important for the hammer pairs.

Course of Fire #3: 25-10 Meters, Timed

5 rounds, single shots from the 25-meter line, in two minutes.

5 rounds, single shots from the 20-meter line, in two minutes.

10 rounds, controlled pairs from the 15-meter line, in two minutes.

10 rounds, hammer pairs from the 10-meter line, in two minutes.

This should be used as your test for basic marksmanship. Any shots left unfired after the time is up are counted as misses. Time begins once you have loaded your pistol, and once it ends, does not begin again until you have loaded for the next string of fire. You should hit at least 90% of your shots to pass.

Course of Fire #4: 15-5 Meters, Untimed

10 rounds, controlled pairs from the 15-meter line.

10 rounds, hammer pairs from the 10-meter line.

15 rounds, hammer pairs and single shots from the 5-meter line.

This is a drill based around stopping an attacker rushing you. If possible, you should set up three targets at the 15, 10, and 5 meter line, and fire one set of shots at each target, from back to front. The 5-meter shots are known as a failure to stop drill, with the hammer pair fired into the torso, then the single shot at either the brain or pelvis, to immediately halt the attacker.

Course of Fire #5: 20 Meters, Untimed

    10 rounds, single shots from the 20-meter line.

    10 rounds, rapid shots from the 20-meter line.

    10 rounds, rapid shots from the 20-meter line.

This is more marksmanship practice. This is more advanced, as you do not have a chance to rest in between each shot while you are making the rapid shots.

Course of Fire #6: 15-5 Meters, Untimed

    10 rounds, controlled pairs from 15-meter line.

    15 rounds, hammer pairs and single shots from the 10-meter line.

    10 rounds, rapid shots from the 5-meter line.

This is to get you used to shooting at close distances. One thing to watch is the difference between point of aim and point of impact. If you zeroed your sights at 25 meters, then the impact may be slightly higher than your aim. The zero will include some bullet drop, so you may need to aim a little lower than usual to hit properly. Pay attention to the difference, so that you know what to expect.

As you train more, you can start adding movement, reloads, malfunction recovery, cover, and multiple targets at once. At the beginning, these are unneeded complications when you need to focus on your marksmanship. Once you have some more experience with your pistol, you can add them in for the sake of realism. Eventually, they will become as much a part of your training as the shooting drills.

When to Shoot

For all the emphasis on shooting and fighting and killing, remember that some fights can only be won if you walk away. Having a pistol and the ability to use it well does not make you invincible. In fact, it can make you even more vulnerable, if you rely on it so much that you forget to stay alert or become overconfident.

A pistol makes a lot of noise each time it time it is fired, and the sound is distinctive. That sound is going to carry, and it will draw attention. After a collapse, a gunshot is going to be a call to all the worst kind of people. Shooting may draw more trouble than it solves.

Getting into a fight is a risk, especially after the collapse. Even when everything is normal, it is dangerous, but it gets much worse if you have no access to medical care. Even a minor injury carries the threat of infection, and major injuries will almost inevitably prove fatal without modern surgery and drugs. If you get hurt, no one is coming for you, except for the ones that hurt you in the first place. Consider that when you are faced with a threat.

In the end, it comes down to your judgment. Every fight is a chance that you might not walk away. On the other hand, shooting when you did not need is less likely to result in your death than not shooting when you should have. The decision, and the consequences, are all on you.

Conclusions

Choosing to arm yourself is a major decision, with implications both now and after any major survival event. Having a weapon, and knowing when and how to use it, could very well be the difference between life and death for you and your family. Of course, as we have seen, it can also be extremely useful for providing food and sustenance now and in a survival situation for you and your family by means of hunting. Those who have a firearm and are well stocked with ammunition will be prepared on an entirely higher level than the general population.

As we've seen, it's extremely important to choose the right firearm for your personal situation. Not everyone will benefit from the same type of firearm so it's important to research which one is best for you before purchasing.

We've also seen that maintenance of your firearm is vital. It's not going to do you any good in a survival situation to have a firearm that you haven't taken care of. It will be of no use to your and your family if you don't properly clean, repair, and maintain the weapon before your life may depend on it. Taking these little steps now will ensure you'll be able to rely on the weapon in the future.

Keeping these things in mind, and learning to use your firearm properly through training exercises and further readings, will put you at an enormous advantage when the you-know-what hits the fan. If you can prepare now, you'll be much better off in the future. And, after all, isn't that what prepping is all about?

Best of luck!

*****

The Frugal Prepper: Survival on a Budget

Prepping is a hobby for some, a lifestyle for many, and a way to make sure that our families are protected should anything happen. "So, what exactly *could* happen?" many people ask. Well, in reality, anything could happen - preppers come from all walks of life and are preparing for vastly different things. Some are simply concerned that a natural disaster might strike where they live and they would not be prepared. Take Hurricane Katrina or the Moore, Oklahoma tornado, for example. Those instances reinforce the fact that natural disasters do happen and, for those that were prepared, they were able to access food and water while FEMA and other rescuers worked on restoring power. For those that were unprepared, well, we saw the worst possible outcomes. You don't want to be one of the ones left behind.

For other people, they are prepping for the end. The Big End. You know who you are. These preppers are serious about doing everything possible to prepare for the worst-case scenario. They may live off the grid, or at least know *how* to, should the need arise, and they teach their entire families to live that way as well. They are the ones that live in more rural areas, where land is cheaper and survival skills are necessary just for their day-to-day lives. Natural disasters happen, doomsday can easily happen and perhaps an economic apocalypse could happen as well. There are many different scenarios that could require us to have prepping and survival skills, so it makes sense to start gathering those skills now, no matter which scenario we think is the most likely.

Today there are millions of individuals and families working feverishly to get prepared for their worst fears or for those events that we all know are coming, sooner or later. They are working hard, and doing very well at it. Prepping is something that, for many people, has become a secret lifestyle. But, regardless of how or why you prep, one of the most common misconceptions about prepping is that it takes a lot of money. Sure, you could spend hundreds of thousands of dollars buying every fancy toy and gadget that claims it will save you and your loved ones. Most of that is just marketing lies. But prepping doesn't have to be that way. Some people become extreme preppers, able to live on very little every month, while others are just accustomed to living frugally. There is a family in Pasadena, California living off 6,000 pounds of produce a year, which all comes from their property. They grow more food than they need and sell the excess to restaurants. Of course, we can't all do that in our situations, but there are always concrete steps that we can take to prep smarter and more cheaply to save money for other purposes.

What is Prepping?

Prepping is simply the action or process of preparing something for use later or preparing *for* something (an event) that may come in the future. Sure, there are those preppers that live on the fringe of society with their thirty-year food pantries, bunkers, and arsenal of mines, bombs, booby traps, grenades, guns, rifles and the like. That's great, if your lifestyle supports that. But for the rest of us, prepping takes time and time is money. What if you need to prep on a budget?

Running to the store last minute to stock up is not an option if you have to collect your family or fortify your home when disaster strikes. Never mind the fact that the rest of city has the same idea. You would be lucky to even make it to the store. The roads would be cluttered, backed up with stop and go traffic. Or worse, they would be blocked off or not usable at all. And even if you make it to the store, the shelves would be cleaned out at best and, at worse, rioting would have already broken out so you wouldn't be able to get the things you need anyways. No, you need a better plan.

Prepping is the best way to give you and your family a good chance to survive any catastrophe. First, you need to know what you are preparing for or against. There are five main factors that lead to death in a survival situation. These are dehydration, starvation, weather, natural situations, and sanitation. To combat these, you'll want to create an emergency pantry composed of water, food, clothes (shoes and blankets too), security (home defense and personal defense), as healthy and clean a living environment as can be provided, and knowledge of various situations and how to best handle those situations. 'Situations' is an all-inclusive term, but could be anything from a spider bite to an angry mob at your front door. 'Situations' can also include mold, illnesses, infections, and depletion of your emergency pantry due to negligence, theft or disaster.

I know what you're thinking: "There are way too many things to possibly be able to plan for!" It can seem overwhelming, certainly, but that's just the start of things. Planning what you want to stock and how you plan to store it is only a third of the battle. Another third of the battle is acquiring knowledge, the proper mindset, and the right skills to succeed in your endeavors. The rest is actually getting the supplies that you need and checking them off of your list to ensure you have everything you need.

Before you start buying up everything in sight, or decide your goal is unobtainable and simply give up, do not get discouraged by the work that lies ahead. Start gradually and aim small. Make a list of the most basic things that you think your family will need to survive. Do some research on this. High profile freeze-dried foods store well and are tasty but they are also very expensive for the average family. And there is no need to buy food that you and your family normally do not consume. The same thing goes for every other category of supply you'll need. But you have to start somewhere, so start with a list of everything you think you'll need. Be as broad as possible, because it's far easier to take things off of the list later, then to try and remember things you have forgotten to add to the list in the first place.

Prepping on a budget is certainly a different way of preparing, because until anything happens at all, the bills keep coming and life goes on. Building a bunker or camping in the wilderness does not provide a steady income like your job does, unfortunately. Finding the time to dedicate to prepping is a challenge because time is money. However, prepping is not just a hobby to do in leisure time. It is a lifestyle, and one that you and your family can adopt without breaking the bank.

Another challenge to prepping on a budget is diligence. Not sticking to your budget with the intent to make it up next week is an example of a common slip up. When you slack in your preparations, it gets easier *to continue to* slack in your preparations. No one is going to sit you down with an intervention when nothing has even happened yet. Rest assured that pointing fingers and the blame game creates enough stress to have you hesitating and second-guessing yourself. Hesitation in a hostile situation could be fatal. Prepping keeps your body, mind, and spirit sharp and fit. For when disaster strikes, it will be too late to "get into shape".

Prepping on a budget takes time and your efforts may seem trivial when you focus on the small, day-to-day items. Yes, it may seem like you are counting pennies, cutting coupons in your free time, and your emergency pantry doesn't look like much. It is easy to give up the plan when nothing appears to have happened. But the little things add up. Before you know it, you'll have more supplies than you realized. And if anything does happen, you and your family will be better fit to survive than if you had done nothing at all.

Prepping on a budget gives you time for trial and error. Learning what foods store well and which ones don't is a part of the process and figuring it out after a disaster usually does not bode well. Prepping on a budget hones your negotiation skills, if you go to flea markets or garage sales for some of your supplies. Other benefits include sharpening your mind and strengthening your resolve. If you have emergency food supplies for 6 months but have no concept of rationing, healthy vs. meager portions, or the self-discipline to stick to the meal rations, then your level of preparedness is not going to be that great. Sticking to a budget will train you to focus on the things that are most important, and this knowledge and way of thinking will seep over into other parts of your life as well, creating even more benefits.

Prepping on a budget usually leads to better budgeting choices in general. You and your family will benefit from prepping on a budget. And it can be a fun experience for a family to do together that doubles as a lifeline. The gradual change is best when including your family and is a preferred method to the culture shock of simply telling or demanding that your family do things a certain way one day, with no reasoning in the build up. Now that you know some challenges and benefits to prepping on a budget, let's look at what you should actually start to prep.

In order to become more independent and build up a self-sustaining prepping habit, there are a few "big picture" things you can start to think of and begin to do to get started, including:

- Become less dependent on your job
- Get out of debt
- Reduce monthly expenses
- Buy some land
- Learn to grow your own food
- Find a reliable source of water nearby or learn how to sterilize water
- Explore alternative energy sources

When you are about to begin your prepping lifestyle, it's important to remember that you should never have to go into debt just because you are prepping. Prepping is about being responsible and that includes paying close attention to your finances. Now is not the time to go into a bunch of debt, simply because you want to have every latest gadget and survival toy. The basics of prepping can be started with little or no money, and these money-saving principles will come back to help you all along your survival way.

To begin your prepping journey, you should always ask yourself: what you are doing this for? What scenarios can you envision happening? And if those happen, what will you need? What is the minimum amount of money or goods that you and your family can survive on? Your family needs to be able to survive, of course, but you don't need to be in debt to prepare for it. Prepping for an unknown future economic reality or otherwise is important. So important that everyone should be able to do it, regardless of their current financial situation.

Once you begin to understand what it is you need to have on hand, it can then become something that you work on to keep you focused and, of course, up to date with your prepping needs. What do you need to have on hand to begin with? It's easy to start. First, understand that you can pick up a few things to begin with as you start your journey to prepperhood. As the months go by, you will begin to notice that your collection will grow, continuously. The more you pick up and store, the longer you'll be able to survive, of course. But it will be fulfilling to see your survival collection grow over the months as you pick up various items when and where it makes most sense to do so.

Prioritizing different areas of your life to become a prepper or survivalist can be wildly successful *if* you stick to a budget and work from it. Chances are, if you have watched any prepping shows, or read any survival blogs, you have seen the massive amounts of items that some people have in their storage areas in case of an emergency. You don't necessarily need to compare yourself to these people. You are not going to need every single thing that they have and the sooner you start tailoring your prepping habits to your family and your specific needs and goals, the easier it will become. You and your family are unique. You have different needs, desires, and abilities than every other family out there. Shouldn't your prepping lifestyle reflect that?

Consider your budget and your family's necessary needs and cut back on items that you obviously don't need. Do you need to dine out every week? Certainly not, and that $30-40 or more could go to your prepping budget. Cable, movies, and other forms of entertainment can be cut back and cut down to allow for more money in your prepping arsenal. You can at least scrounge between $300-400 a month extra for prepping in this manner. Then, after your have worked on your budget and have started to save money, you can start actually buying what you need!

What to Prep

In the interest of gradually transitioning to a prepper lifestyle, it's best to start out with an Every Day Carry (EDC). An EDC refers to those items that you carry on you throughout the day. Of course you will have your phone, car keys, and wallet, but, in terms of prepping, decide which other items would benefit you in any situation. In addition to what you already carry, here is a good place to start:

- Pocket Knife, Multitool, or Swiss Army Knife

- Para-cord Survival Bracelet

- A lighter (Windproof is better)

- Watch

These items are lightweight and can even be carried in a cigarette case or aluminum wallet for consolidation. The idea is to help you help yourself. It's not a rescue mission, but these items can help you get yourself into a better position for a rescue mission. Another important point to note is that these items should stay on your person at all times. They do not stay in your car, on your desk, in the jacket pocket of the coat you just hung up, or in your purse. If you're going to be able to use them, they need to be with you, so get in the habit of keeping your EDC on you at all times.

The next step in prepping that you will want to consider is creating a Bug Out Bag (BOB). A BOB is designed to aid you in getting out of the way of danger as quickly and efficiently as possible. If a tornado touches down nearby while you're driving, outrunning it may not be an option. You may have to leave the car and head for safety. You may be close to home or you may be nowhere near your home. But, with a bug out bag, you will have food, water, and other items to aid you in toughing out the storm, or any other survival situation you may find yourself in. So, what goes in your Bug Out Bag, exactly? Well, first off, you will want to start with a large backpack to put it all in. One that fits well, is comfy and easy to carry, but with enough storage to fit all the items you want to carry. Here are some items for you and your family to include:

Nutrition:

- Meal Replacement Bars for 24 hours to 72 hours. That's 3-10 bars per person, roughly.

- Bottle of Water for each meal (3-10 bottles, per person)

Supplies:

- Pocketknife, Combat Knife or Multitool

- Waterproof Matches, Lighter, and maybe Cottons Ball soaked in Petroleum Jelly (highly flammable)

- First Aid Kit, Sewing Kit, Flashlight, Batteries

- Toilet Paper, Sunscreen, Bug Spray

- Spare personal medicine or prescription glasses (if you wear glasses)

Defense:

- Stun Gun, Baton, Pepper Spray

General:

- Spare Change of Clothes Including socks and underwear

- Toothbrush/Baking Soda

- Tarp, Para-cord Bracelet, Sleeping Bag, Blankets, Handwarmers

These items will meet your basic needs for one to three days (depending on how many days you prepare for). They will also aid in giving you more time to find help or get yourself in a better position as far as nutrition, shelter and situations go. Keep bug out bags for all members of your family, as creating one is a great way to get your kids involved and invested in their future as well.

Bug Out Bags can also be kept in your home in addition to in your vehicle. Even if you fortify your home, you may still find yourself in a compromising position where leaving your home is a wiser decision than staying. Repeat the BOB process and create one for your vehicle as well as your home. That way, no matter if you stay or go, you'll have access to your BOB and a few extra days of survival. Again, ensure that each member in your party has a bug out bag prepared.

Ways to Cut Costs

Food and water is a huge part of survival, obviously. Without it, we don't even stand a chance. Acquiring what you need can be broken down into three questions: 1) How many months do you want your emergency pantry to last? 2) What is the minimum amount that you and your family need? 3) How much is your family's budget?

The important thing to remember about prepping on a budget is to simply take the next step. Don't get caught up in the huge end picture all of the time. Focus on what you can do today, you're your first step will be, and work to achieve that. Even if you start out with buying just one extra can of food a week, it is one extra can in your emergency pantry. If that is all that you can manage for the next year, by the end of that year, you will have 52 cans in your emergency pantry. Not bad at all.

One way to save money while building your emergency pantry is to cut coupons for the items that are on your list. This is something that your family can participate in. Another way to save money is to become a rewards customer. Many major and minor grocery stores have a rewards cards or clubs that reward shoppers with gift cards, savings in fuel, or special club discounts. You can couple your club discounts with your coupons and get near double the savings. Do some research on which stores carry the products that you need and find coupons for those items. Some grocery stores even have online coupons that you can access in the store or you can have them emailed to you. Thrift stores are another way to build up your emergency pantry. Many thrift stores have 1/2 off sales pretty regularly. That's the time to shop. Again, remember your list and your budget and stick to it. Visit different thrift stores for what you need.

Buying supplies in bulk can create huge savings. If you purchase a case of canned goods and that total equals your prepping budget for the month, you might think it's a bad idea at first. But, remember, you won't need to purchase any more canned goods after that month, and can focus on other items from your list. Use your time and money wisely. Research the other items on your list and get your coupons ready. See what's on sale this week or this month and focusing on knocking those items off of your list.

Networking with other people in your mindset can provide information and tips to help you and your family in your task.

Last but not least, learn to fix, patch, reuse and re-task. Patching up clothes and fixing tools or equipment is an invaluable skill that will more than come in handy should you have to delve into your survival pantry. And, when you cannot fix or patch an item, re-task it. Just about anything can be multipurpose. It's a good idea to do some research and get hands-on experience with building and repairing. You can even visit some workshops or free seminars on this subject. You don't have to be an expert in everything and anything, but it helps to have some idea of where to begin.

Building a Survival Food Pantry on a Budget

Prices of everything are going up, and our earnings are drastically down across most every industry. For some of us, this means that we are living on the edge of poverty, striving to pay our bills and get through each week, living paycheck to paycheck. Food and supplies are the first thing we need to survive. The shelves in any store are stocked, but in an instant, when a natural disaster or another emergency strikes, those shelves will be emptied. Losing your job, having a personal crisis, or a national tragedy can affect your ability to feed your family and yourself. Grocery stores have stocks of food right now, but that can change as well. They used to have larger warehouse areas that had the ability to keep restocking, but most stores these days are limited to a 3-day supply of goods. That's including the stock that they have in the back. If anything happened to the trucks or the ships coming with food, then the grocery stores will run out. That's if there is not already a huge surge in people buying before a crisis, which we have seen in past disasters is almost always the case.

What would happen today if you could not leave your home? Would you have enough food to last a week? What about a month? If the answer is yes, then congratulations - you are doing a great prepping job. You are also one of the few prepared ones. But, if the answer is no, then you are not living off-grid or prepping at all. You need to do this, for you and your family, and you need to make sure that you have the food in the pantry starting this week. If you have extra food, it should be enough for at least two weeks minimum, but you don't need to go overboard and stock a year's worth of food right away. This will ensure you will not have to choose between buying food and paying a mortgage.

Decide first - how much money can you spend? And if you do not have a budget for food prepping, then start looking at where your money goes. Stretch your earnings, and look at what you are spending your money on. For instance, do you really, really need that $4.00 cup of joe from the local high-priced coffee shop? No, I think not. Do you need the junk food? No, you don't. Can you cook from scratch and save money? Yes, though it may not save time, it will most certainly save you money in the long run.

When building your pantry, you will want enough food for you and your family to eat everyday for at least 6 to 12 months. There are emergency pantry calculators online that help you calculate your family's minimum food storage needs. For a family of 4, a 6-month emergency pantry is usually suggested as follows:

600 lbs. of Grain – This includes rice, oats, corn meal, wheat, and flour.

26 lbs. of Fats – These come in the form of cooking oils, shortening, and peanut butter

120 lbs. of Beans & Peas – This includes Pinto, Lima, and Soy beans. It also includes, peas,   dry soup mix, and legumes.

300 lbs. of Cooking Essentials – Essentials means honey, sugar, jams, dehydrated   milk, evaporated milk, baking soda, baking powder, salt, vinegar, and water.

The emergency pantry calculator can be a starting point for your pantry and help guide you and your family towards storing enough food for 6 months. When beginning an emergency pantry, keep in mind that the numbers used to calculate the pounds of food for storage are based on the average minimum amount of 1200-calorie consumption daily. It's not a hard rule but there are side effects to meager meals. Starvation leaves the person sluggish with little energy. The muscles begin to atrophy without protein to keep them strong. Fatigue and weight loss of lean muscle are major effects of not eating enough and are detrimental to survival of any situation. The goal is to stay as healthy as possible while rationing your pantry, so you may want to up those baseline amounts if you plan on eating over 1200 calories per person, per day.

When building an emergency pantry, remember to also store water. Easy to forget, but a deadly mistake if you do. Most food expands in the stomach when coupled with water. This helps to digest the food and gives a feeling of fullness. The foods that you prepare may also require water, of course, yet this is one area that preppers often overlook. You can purchase 5 gallon jugs, 1 liter bottles, cases of water or create your own water storage system, just so long as you have what your and your family needs. You will need it to cook, to drink, to wash your clothes, and to wash yourself. Keep this in mind as your begin your emergency food pantry.

The foods that you want to stockpile the most are the ones that are protein rich and provide the most nutritional bang for their buck. Unopened boxes or bags of cereal are safe to consume for up to 8 months and make for a quick light breakfast. Foods high in energy and protein such as peanut butter, nuts and granola bars are a great addition to any emergency pantry. Dehydrated fruits are also protein rich and last anywhere from 6 months to 1 year. Below are a few ideas of the main types of foods you will want to start stocking:

Canned Soups – Ready-to-eat soups can often be eaten without heating. Pour some water in and you're ready to go. Sure, we're used to them hot, but the same nutrients are there, regardless of the temperature. There are many varieties such as vegetable, beef, chicken, tomato and more. Many ready-to-eat canned soups are also manufactured with an easy quick-pop lid that doesn't require a can opener. This includes canned chili. Look for those and you'll be good.

Canned fruits and vegetables – Stock up on canned pasta sauce, green beans, peas, carrots, corn, grapefruit, oranges, and any other of your preferred fruits and vegetables. These canned vegetables have a shelf life of up to 3 years and still remain nutritious with protein, vitamins, and antioxidants.

Canned meats – These include tuna, chicken, spam, and salmon. Meat will be in short supply either because the grocery markets have been ransacked or because there's no longer any meat production. Meat is a source of iron and protein. Buy in bulk and buy on sale. Typically have a very long shelf life so you can feel safe buying in bulk to store.

Pasta – Pasta has little water content and stores for up to 2 years in a cool, dark space in an airtight container. Pasta provides for a quick meal. You can improvise by adding canned meat and vegetables to get a nutritious and filling dinner. Avoid stockpiling pastas with egg because this type of pasta has a small amount of fat in it that can break down over time and begin to smell and spoil.

Dehydrated Potatoes – These have a shelf life of a couple years. Be aware of the fact that some instant mashed potatoes mixes add butter and dry milk for flavor, resulting in a reduced shelf life.

Packaged meals – Ramen noodles, macaroni and cheese, and dinner pasta mixes are a good way to mix up the meals so that you and your family aren't eating the same drab meal night after night. Add variety with your canned meats and vegetables.

One thing you don't want to forget in your emergency pantry is cooking spices and ingredients such as vinegar, baking powder, or baking soda. You can even include chicken, beef, and vegetable bouillon cubes. They don't take up a lot of room and help create soups and stews. For your cooking oils, you will want to store vegetable-based oils. These are oils such as olive oil, coconut oil, and vegetable oil. They won't spoil for years, unlike some animal-based oils. An emergency pantry isn't about eating excruciatingly obnoxious survival food, astronaut food, or any other kind of food, except for what you and your family normally eat. When you are deciding which food to buy in bulk, consider its shelf life as well. The following foods store the longest and are a cost-efficient addition to any emergency pantry:

Corn Meal – 12-month shelf life.

Peppercorns – 1-3 years shelf life.

Powdered Milk – 2 years normally, but if kept at a cool 40 degrees Fahrenheit will last up to 10 years.

Regular Sugar-Free 1 Minute or 5 Minute Oatmeal – 2-3 years

Dried Split Peas – 4-5 years (will last indefinitely with O2 Absorbers in an airtight container – more on those below)

Vitamins – 4-5 years shelf life.

1200 to 3600 Calorie Food Bars - 5 years

These food bars are relatively inexpensive calorie ration food bars that are packed with nutrition and are great for your pantry or Bug Out Bags. The trick to getting the savings is to buy in bulk. A 72-hour supply is usually ten dollars at the most. But a 20-day supply is sold for up to 33% off in savings.

Rolled Oats – Up to 28 years when stored oxygen free. Portion your oats into airtight plastic containers with oxygen absorbers to allow for maximum shelf life, easier usage, and rotation.

White Rice – 4-5 years. Oxygen free white rice will last 25-30 years. Again, portion your rice into airtight plastic containers with oxygen absorbers to allow for maximum shelf life, easier usage, and rotation.

Dried Pinto Beans and Lentils– Indefinite. They are a great source of high protein, vitamins, and fiber while being low maintenance, low fat and low cost.

Honey – Indefinite. Honey also has medicinal application because of its antibacterial activity.

Sugar – Indefinite

Salt – Indefinite

While they aren't necessary for your pantry, oxygen absorbers are most definitely prudent and can significantly extend the shelf life of your stored foods. Oxygen absorbers can mean a difference of decades in terms of shelf life. Oxygen can cause mold, spoilage, nutritional oxidation, condensation, and attract bugs. It's not enough to quickly store food; even in an already airtight container, oxygen is already in there. The solution is to invest in oxygen absorbers.

Oxygen absorbers are little pouches of iron oxide. They aren't edible but they are safe to use around your food, don't leak toxins, and don't alter your food in any way. The oxygen absorbers are measured in "CC" or "cubic centimeters". So, a 2000cc oxygen absorber will absorb 2000 cubic centimeters of oxygen. The general rule is to use 2000cc of oxygen absorbers per 5-gallon bucket. Oxygen makes up about 21% of air and the right amount of oxygen absorbers can take that percentage down to .01%.

Some preppers will even store rice and beans in 2 liter beverage bottles. They are food safe and colored plastics can help protect against light exposure, which also break down stored foods. Just add an oxygen absorber or two and tighten the lid.

5-gallon food grade buckets can be purchased in sets of 3-5 buckets for $20 to $25 online. You can get 10 Mylar Bags for 5-gallon buckets and a quantity of 10 Oxygen Absorbers at 2000cc a piece for $20 to $30 online. Just be sure to check the bags for leaks before filling them. A good way to do this is to shine a flashlight in the bags, in a dark room.

Oxygen absorbers are packaged in an airtight plastic. Once broken, the absorbers will start to absorb. So, it is practical to have your buckets or 2-liters or storage container already filled with food before opening the oxygen absorbers. Never leave oxygen absorbers out for more than 30 minutes or they will expire. Insert them into the food and close the container airtight. The remaining absorbers can be kept in another airtight container, such as a Mason jar. Fill it up with rice to reduce the amount of oxygen in the jar.

Back to acquiring your emergency pantry foods: gardening can be a fun, family affair and it's a good way to get your family involved in preparedness. Growing your own food is a useful skill that puts you and your family one step closer to your goal and far ahead of the average family these days. One thing to consider when gardening is to only grow foods that your family actually eats. Another thing to consider is that you want to grow foods that produce more than one vegetable or fruit per plant or produces more than one harvest.

Here are a few vegetables that are easy to grow and some tips to help you along the way:

Carrots are easy to plant. They grow underground and don't require a bunch of fuss. You can even grow them in pots; just make sure the pot is deep enough. When the carrot tops come through the soil, they are ready to harvest.

Lettuce and Spinach have many different varieties to choose from and are easy to maintain. Lettuce is partial to cooler weather so planting in the spring or fall is adequate. Sow new seeds every 2 to 3 weeks to spread out your harvest.

Tomato plants only need a bit of water and lots of sun. They will grow all summer long and continue to produce fruit as well.

Sweet potatoes are very resilient. They can be grown in imperfect soil and hot weather. Wait about one month after the last freeze to give the ground time to warm up.

Bush beans are another great and easy to plant vegetable for your garden. Some well-drained soil and a lot of sun make for the perfect bed for sowing. Once again, continue to sow seeds every 2-3 weeks to keep a continuous harvest going.

Seeds are inexpensive to buy and these easy-to-grow foods don't require hours of care or any special type of fertilizer. When considering storage options, vegetables and meats can be canned at home using a pressure canner. Pressure canning is method used to preserve food low in acid. This includes meats, poultry, fish, chili, and vegetables. It's similar to regular canning with the added element of pressure that depends on your altitude. The pressure is very important to processing low-acidic or alkaline foods at a higher temperature. The bacteria botulism dies at the boiling water temperature, but its spores may survive. So, the extra added pressure heats the water to a higher temperature. It is for this reason, when canning vegetables, meats, and fish, that a pressure canner, which is different from a pressure cooker, is used and used right.

Pressure cookers cost $100 and upwards and may be out of your budget range now and in the foreseeable future. Another option for your vegetable harvests is that you and your family can sell leftover produce from your garden and put the money saved towards your emergency pantry.

Canning with fruits and tomatoes or tomatoes sauce (which is actually a fruit) may be a more cost effective canning option for your budget. Ball Regular-Mouth Mason jars with lids and bands can be purchased in cases of 12 anywhere from $10 and upwards. The canned goods can be stored safely in your pantry for at least 1 year, so long as they are used before 2 years.

Waterbath canning is a time-tested process that has been used for ages. This method can be used to can fruits, jams, jellies, applesauce, salsa, and tomatoes. This process requires a large stockpot, at least 7 1/2 inches in height and 9 1/2 wide. Fill it with enough water to cover the mason jars by an inch and boil. Wash your mason jars, lids and bands. Warming up the jars in hot dishwater eliminates the chance of breakage when they are filled with hot foods.

The recipes used for preparing your fruits, jams, jellies or pickles range from varieties that include Pectin (a gelling agent) to those that don't include Pectin or any other agents. As long as the concoction remains acidic, you can use the waterbath process while being creative. Once your food is prepared, add it to the Mason jars, leaving about an inch of headspace. Stir and smash the food to each side of the Mason jar to remove bubbles. After you wipe the rims of the jars, center the lid on the top of the Mason jar and apply the band until it is fingertip tight. This allows ample room for air bubbles to escape during the waterbath. Insert the filled and topped mason jars into the stockpot and keep the water at least an inch above the Mason jar. Put the stockpot lid back on the pot. Your recipe will have an amount of time to let the jars boil. Remember to take into account your altitude. Basically, add 5 minutes for every 3,000 feet that you are above sea level.

After boiling the jars for the appropriate amount of time, remove from heat and let the jars stand 5 minutes. Then remove the jars, keeping them upright, and place them on a rack or kitchen towel and counter to cool. You want the jars to cool for 8 to 12 hours to complete the process and complete the seal. After 8 to 12 hours, test the seal by pushing it with your finger. If it rebounds, then the jar isn't sealed properly. Another way to test the seal is to tap the bottom of the jar with a teaspoon. If the sound is dull, the jar may not be sealed properly. What you're listening for is a high-pitched ring. The last way to test the seal is to view the seal at eye level. If it isn't concave (caved it), but it is flat or bulging, then the jar may not be sealed properly. If an improper seal is the case, the canned goods can still be refrigerated and used by you and your family, but should not be stored for extended periods of time.

You may experience variations in color or consistency in your home canned products. That doesn't mean that the products are dangerous for consumption. Know what normal home canning variations look like. A brown color or darker color is typically caused by oxidation or a breakdown in the color of the food, as in the case of apples or guacamole. Soft texture in food is caused by a breakdown in food or plant tissue due to heat. Crystals in canned fish is a result of pressure canning Magnesium Ammonium Phosphate, which is in fish. Crystals in fruits are caused by a high acidic salt compound but they are still safe to consume. Metal cans (some people still home-can goods with actual cans) may leave bits of metal or a metallic taste on the food. And, when the food is above the juice line in the jar, it is still safe for consumptions as long as the seal remains intact.

Signs of bad jars or cans are if it's badly dented, leaking or rusting. If the jar or can has a broken seal or it spurts upon opening, then the food inside has been compromised. As a general rule of common sense, always inspect the jar or can with your eyes and nose. If there is a strange odor or appearance, then discard it – it's not worth the risk to the health of you and your family.

When building your emergency pantry, you will also want to consider vitamin-infused powder, purchased in bulk when possible. Seeds are another item that you may want to keep in supply. It would be handy should your emergency pantry deplete before your situation resolves.

Trade and bartering may come in handy in a world where supermarkets no longer exist. Letting your family try their bartering skills at a flea market is one way to get them involved in preparedness. Another way to get your family involved is to have them cut coupons for fruits (to can) when they are on sale and getting them involved in a relatively inexpensive ($30 or less) canning process. When storing your successfully canned goods, remember to label them with the date made, the ingredients, and the expiration date.

How the food is stored is an important part of maintaining your emergency pantry. You will want an easy-to-understand inventory system that allows for easy rotation of foods. You can achieve this. Label all cans, jars, buckets, and bags with the date acquired or date manufactured, and the expiration date, and ingredients. You want your emergency pantry to remain at cool consistent temperature and a dark, dry space. Teach your family the labeling system so that everyone can easily know how to read the labels and determine what is safe to eat.

Water

As mentioned before, five common factors of death in a survival situation are dehydration, starvation, weather, situations, and sanitation. Dehydration is when the body needs water and doesn't have it. It is one of the quickest forms of death in a survival situation, and one of the most easily avoidable. Some symptoms are:

- Increased thirst, dry mouth, and swollen tongue

- Inability to sweat, decreased or concentrated urine output

- Weakness, dizziness, fatigue and fainting

- Diarrhea, fever, headaches, and seizures

When storing emergency water, allot each person in your plan one gallon per day. So for a family of 4, you would need four gallons of water for each day you plan for. For 6 months, that amounts to 745 gallons of water. And, that's just for consumption, not even taking into account the water you need for cooking, bathing, and cleaning.

How does one go about collecting 750 gallons of water? One idea is to collect rainwater. Rainwater collection has been around for centuries. It is used even by states that are known to have deserts and those that experience severe droughts. One square foot of rain on the average roof in certain climates can amount to 600 gallons of water per year, if collected properly. If you have gutters, you can divert the water already collected on your roof into your water storage barrels via your gutters. Invest in a gutter filter to prevent leaves, sticks, and other debris from clogging up your system. You will want 2-4 food grade water barrels connected via hose adapters and a hose. The extra water barrels serve as an overflow system once the first barrel is full. Some people even add an extra hose to the last barrel in the chain and position the hose downhill and away from their home. This ensures that any extra overflow diverts downhill and doesn't collect in the basement of their home.

When collecting rainwater, understand that it may still need filtering and purification before being fit to drink. Another thing to consider when collecting rainwater is that you may need a permit in some counties and states, or it may be illegal altogether (crazy, I know!). Do your research and know your facts and the law to avoid being caught up in the system. That's valuable time that you could be investing towards you and your family's survival plan.

The barrels used for water storage should be food grade. Yes, this was already mentioned, but it is vitally important, so I'm mentioning it again. The barrels specifically manufactured for water storage come with a spout, leaf filter, and overflow value and can be purchased at your local hardware store, online, and at gardening supply stores. Water barrels range from 55 gallons to 75 gallons and cost anywhere from $80 to $200. You can buy them with the spigot or without. The barrels without spigots can be converted using a few tools and parts. You can also negotiate with food manufacturers and large restaurants for their used 55-gallon food grade barrels. Make sure that you clean them well. If the barrel was used for storing oil or any type of chemical, pass on it. It'll be really tough to clean thoroughly and you don't want to gamble with you or your family's safety.

Another method for collecting water for storage is to invest in tub bladders. These cost as low as $20 and are great in case of an emergency. It's as simple as placing the heavy-duty plastic bladder in the tub, connecting it to the spout, and turning on the water. The tub contains the bladder and the bladder fills up within a few minutes. The bladder keeps the water clean and holds up to 100 gallons drinking water. The bladder is even fitted with a siphon pump for when you need to use the water.

You can even get creative with placing these tub bladders in a 55-gallon drum or tub-like homemade structure and running a hose from your tub to the bladder. It's effectively stored in a food grade container and provides clean drinking water at your disposal. It's inexpensive. It would keep your tub clear and it wouldn't require you to move 100 gallons of water. The cost would be the price of the bag, the cost of the container or bladder-holding structure and the normal cost of taking a bath. The water stored in tub bladders will be useable for up to 4 weeks. Utilizing an air compressor, you can flush the pump, nozzle and bladder in a light bleach solution that will keep the bladder cleaner and ready for re-use. Many tub bladders are expected to be single use. So if you find an air compressor on sale, make the investment and save some money.

Some common challenges to water storage are algae, mosquitoes, and clogged spigots. Algae grow as a response to light warming up the water. You can avoid this by adding 1/8 teaspoon to 1/4 teaspoon of unscented regular household bleach per gallon to your water storage. Store the water in a cool, dark place, and keep it covered. Most food grade water barrels are designed to keep out light.

Mosquitoes like to lay eggs in stagnant water. Keeping your water covered is your best defense against mosquitoes and their larvae. Other ways to combat mosquito larvae is to cover the intake with nylon pantyhose. You will need to check the filter often to ensure that the pantyhose don't have any holes at all and isn't deteriorating. The nylon pantyhose is fine enough a filter to keep out mosquitoes seeking to lay eggs but will still allow water to pass through. However, the pantyhose require diligence because the smallest hole will allow mosquitoes.

Another way to combat mosquito larvae is to use Mosquito Dunks. Mosquito Dunks are small ringed products containing the bacteria BTI. It's only toxic to mosquito larvae, lasts 30 days, and treats 100 square feet of water. These rings have an indefinite shelf life so long as they remain dry and unused. You can purchase a 6 pack of Mosquito Dunks for a little as $10. And, Mosquito Dunks can be halved and quartered for use in smaller areas.

The third common problem with water storage is clogged spigots and low water pressure. Here's a simple fix for that. Remove the top of the spigot with a pair of pliers. Water should squirt out due to the pressure release. If this doesn't happen, then use a twig, stick or pipe cleaner to clear the flow path until the water squirts out, clearing the rest of the way. If a clogged filter is also resulting in low pressure, this will rectify that situation. Sometimes low water pressure is caused by low water levels in your storage unit. When you have more water in your water storage unit, you will have better water pressure because the water is creating the pressure. But, the less water you have in your storage unit, the less pressure your will have.

Knowledge of whether water can be made into potable drinking water is important because you don't want to waste your resources on a lost cause. There are ways to filter and purify water for these purposes. A few common ways are boiling, bleach, potable water purification tabs and filters.

Boiling is a great way to remove dangerous bacteria from your water, as is 1/8 teaspoon to 1/4 teaspoon of regular unscented household liquid bleach. In water purification tablets (50 tablets cost about $10), the active ingredient is usually chlorine or iodine and the tablets are another great way to deactivate bacteria, viruses, and parasites. However, water purification tablets do not remove chemicals or sediment from the water nor does it kill Cryptosporidium, which can cause diarrhea. It would be a last step after filtering your water. Filters can be purchased for your water storage or for emergency use in your bug out bag or you can make your own filter.

When you begin making your filter, you will want coffee filters, activated charcoal (2 bottles cost about $10 to $12), rinsed sand, and rinsed gravel (small pebbles or stones). You can use two 5-gallon buckets, or a 2-liter soda bottle for this purpose. Some people even create a larger filtering system using a 5-gallon bucket per ingredient and connecting them through plastic plumbing fittings.

Poke or cut holes in the bottom of the container that will be the actual filter. More small holes as opposed to few large holes are preferable. Insert the coffee filters in the bottom of the container. On top of the coffee filter, place a layer of activated charcoal. Follow that with a layer of sand and another layer of activated charcoal. For your next layer, add another layer of sand and follow that layer with a layer of gravel. Your filter is now complete.

After you pour your water through the filter, check the water for sediment or cloudiness. You may have to pour it through a second time. Next, aerate (put air back into your water) the water by pouring it back and forth from each pitcher or bucket.

The first layer of gravel removes large debris like pebbles, sticks, leaves, bugs, and the like. The sand filters out finer particles too small to be caught by the gravel layer. The layer of activated carbon removes, by absorption, bacteria and some chemicals. This bio-filter can be made quickly and on a smaller scale when you are on the move. Or you can make a larger filter for your water reserve as you use it.

Your family can be involved by calling food manufacturers and large restaurants for 55 gallon food grade barrels. You can have younger children collect pebbles or sand for the filter and rinse them. You family also can help you by building rain catchers or tub bladder units if they are old enough.

When you are prepping on a budget, food and water are very important sections of your emergency pantry but there's more. You'll want to make a list of tools and supplies you will need such as clothing, sanitation supplies, light, fire, or electricity, and tools to help you get the job done and defend your shelter. More on those below...

Clothing

When building an emergency pantry, one very important factor that you need to prep for is different types of weather. You don't want you and your family to find yourselves with a 6-month supply of food and water and no spare clothing. You will want to stock a quality pair of waterproof work boots per member in your party, perhaps an extra pair in a larger size if you still have growing children.

A plethora of cheap, comfortable socks and underwear will keep you and your family with fresh dry undergarments. It might seem like a small thing, but believe me, when you are wet and trying to survive day-to-day, clean, dry undergarments can mean the difference between sanity and losing your mind! If you keep wet clothes and shoes on, you can catch any number of diseases. Of course, the common cold, pneumonia, and the like. One not-so-known problem is trench feet. Trench feet is a condition caused by overexposure to damp, cold, wet, unsanitary conditions, poor circulation, and not allowing your feet to dry. People who have had it in the past are mostly likely to encounter it again. Characteristics of trench feet may be swelling, turning red or blue, or a putrid odor, like decay. More advanced symptoms include open sores, blisters, and fungal infections. If left untreated, gangrene can develop. Wouldn't it be easier to avoid all of that and just pack an extra pair of dry socks? Yes!

As with socks and underwear, you will want to stock shirts and pants. Some opt for quantity over quality, if they have extra room. Some prefer to shell out a bit more money upfront for one or two really well-made items, in hopes they will last longer. The choice is up to you. Cotton-blend is always a good choice. They are comfortable and retain a decent look and feel over multiple periods of wearing. You will also want to invest in some rain gear for you and your family. This time you want to stick with quality over quantity. You don't want a water resistant anything. You want a durable waterproof nylon jacket with treated rip-proof seams and a hood. You want the same quality in rain pants that can be worn over clothing, boots and all for each member in your party, particularly if you're in a climate zone with frequent rainfall.

Make sure to include thermal undershirts and underpants for warmth and shorts and short sleeve t-shirts for hot days. Heat stroke is very common and can be a reoccurring nuisance. Only store clean clothes and label the storage unit or box for each member in your party for some organization. Don't forget to stock up on diapers if you have small children, but wait till they graduate to a new diaper size. This gives you a greater chance of having the right size diaper should disaster strike.

One way that you and your family can save money in this area is utilizing thrift shops on their 1/2 off sale days. At thrift stores, you can find gently used work books, jumpsuits, and more. Learning to repair fabric and materials will be a key factor in making your clothing and materials last. You and your family can even repair your current clothing when it tears and add it to your emergency pantry. You can often find items in thrift stores that people got rid of simply because they didn't want to bother making a few stiches or hems. If you can learn to do some simple repairs, you'll save yourself a ton of money in the long run.

If you are going to repair clothing, you need to stock up on materials to repair with. Sewing kits, zipper repairs, needles, thread, and yarn is a good starting point. For repairing shoes, you'll want to invest in shoe repair kits, heel savers, and sewing awls (for heavy duty fabrics). In the event that the emergency situation isn't resolved within 6 months, investing in yourself by learning to make clothes with a sewing machine, knitting, or crochet is a vital skill that you can barter with.

Now, what about doing laundry? If you do decide on a power generator for your home, you might be tempted with a washer and dryer, and while that method is a faster way to do laundry, it guzzles water, energy, and breaks down clothing faster. Some ways to keep clothing lasting longer is to line dry clothes. Treat stains right away with a stain removing solution. Store only clean clothes and avoid storing clothes in moisture or mildew. Stains and body oils and fluids (like sweat) attract moths and bugs and moisture and mildew break down clothing. Storing clothes with baking soda can help reduce moisture and mildew.

Sanitation and First Aid

Besides starvation and dehydration, sanitation will be one of the leading killers in a disaster. There are some supplies you can acquire that will lessen you and your family's chance of falling victim to disease. First things first: pay attention to scrapes, cuts, bumps, and bruises, and take care of them before they go any further. Isopropyl alcohol and hydrogen peroxide are must have items as an antiseptic. Chances are that any first aid kit will contain antiseptic wipes but, for the long haul, you will want to stock several bottles of each.

If anyone in your party needs special medications or inhalers, you will want to acquire extra beforehand. This can be a difficult task considering the regulations on medication and you may have to speak with your doctor about your options. Other items in this category include hearing aids and extra batteries, or prescription glasses. Most people will overlook having extra of these items in case of emergency; don't be one of those people!

In your first aid kit, whether you buy a prepackaged one or custom make your own, you will want at least a few of these items, if not all of them:

Rolls of gauze with the fasteners: these are useful for sprains, and covering bandaging

Tweezers: Useful for splinters, ticks, and more

Medical scissors (pointed & sharp): Used for removing stitches

Medical scissors (blunt): Used for removing bandages without damaging surrounding skin.

Skin glue: Closing up surface wounds and acts as a liquid Band-Aid

Cotton swabs and cotton balls: Used for cleaning wounds and applying antiseptics, cream, or   ointments

Eye drops: Used for lubricating eyeball

Aspirin is important medicine to stock in your emergency pantry. Aspirin can halt a heart attack because it dilutes the blood and allows for easier passage through the heart. But it doesn't take the place of a doctor so if you can reach a doctor, that would be your best bet. Aspirin also reduces swelling because it's an anti-inflammatory drug in addition to reducing fevers and minor aches and pains.

Of course, for ointments and creams, you want antibiotic ointment to stave off infection and hydrocortisone cream for bug bites, rashes, and run-ins with poison ivy and poison oak. Last but not least, hand sanitizer will come in handy should you have to patch up yourself or others.

For the sake of cleanliness, here are a few items that you and your family should stock and will definitely benefit from:

Cat Litter: I know, I know. You don't have a cat so why in the world would you want to stock cat litter? Well, it's a really useful tool! Soaks like a sponge and it's useful for human waste or biofluids gone awry. It can help reduce mold or moisture from water and soak up any other type of liquid spill.

Bleach: Useful for purifying water and cleaning. Bleach expires and is poisonous in large doses. Use caution in storage & rotation in your pantry and always adhere to directions for usage.

Baking Soda: Use as a toothpaste, deodorizer, cleaning agent and fire extinguisher.

Vinegar: Use as cleaner & deodorizer. Vinegar effectively eliminates cat urine and skunk sprays.

Three 5-Gallon Buckets or Dishpans for cleaning dishes: Use a bucket each to scrape food into, wash dishes, and sanitize dishes.

Body soap, dishwashing soap, sponge, and towels: Soap to clean yourself and your dishes. Use separate towels for dishes and bodies and each member in your party should have their own towel

Facial tissues, toilet paper, washable handkerchiefs, and paper-towels: These help reduce the spread of germs as long as they are properly stored.

Sanitary Napkins: They can also double as a sterile medical pad for a wound.

Electricity, Light, and Fire

You're going to need some electricity and light in a survival situation; that much is a given. How willing are you to rely on your local grid staying online? How comfortable are you without electricity? Some light sources that you'll want to consider are batteries, lamps and oil, and creating your own electricity. Batteries will store for about 2 years in an extremely humid environment but in a dry environment, they will last anywhere from 4 to 6 years. Refrigerated batteries stored in an airtight zip lock bag will last from 6 to 9 years and batteries stored in a freezer will last for 10 years or more. These numbers vary upon the humidity and the temperature, and the quality of battery used. Rechargeable batteries, however, work best at room temperature. Batteries are a prudent investment for emergencies and from the initial emergency till you have time to get situated.

Oil lamps, while they can start fires if dropped, are still a better alternative to candles. With candles, the open flame can start fires with curtains or anything else that gets in its way. The candle can blow out when you need it the most and candles don't actually provide that much light. Oil lamps are brighter than candles and they can be purchased with a light reflector to amplify the light as well. Most oil lamps have a wind guard to protect the flame from going out and they are easier to maneuver due to their sturdy base and handle.

For electricity, your options will be limited to your budget or do-it-yourself skill set. Generators start from $630 for a propane-powered generator or $650 for an oil-powered generator and go way, way higher from there. There are, of course, do-it-yourself resources available for building your own power generators from solar, wind, and water and if you have any handyman skills, these could be a very useful, economical alternative. When considering whether or not to invest in a generator, consider what you will be using it for. You and your family's energy consumption will be significantly reduced in the case of a hunker-down emergency. Nevertheless, electricity may be another component of your preparation that you may want to focus on after your more important and basic supplies are gathered. You might consider low payment layaway plans for purchasing a generator, if you decide that having a steady supply of electricity is essential for your family's plans.

If you plan to make fire, then you need to stock up on items like charcoal, firewood, lighter fluid and tinder. For your lamps, you'll need lamp oil, wicks and the lamps. You can store two lamps to use and have 2 backup or emergency lamps. You may need more lamps for a larger family, of course. Cotton balls soaked in petroleum jelly make for a quick, inexpensive fire starter as well. While candles are not ideal, some light is better than none at all, so add candles and candle holders to your pantry, as a type of backup to your backup plan. The non-scented candles will attract less attention from bugs and people. As for the fire itself, you will want different ways to create fire, of course. Learn fire-starting techniques if you don't know any already. Teach your spouse, children, and anyone else that will be surviving with you. Stock up on matches, lighters, magnesium and flint starters, waterproof matches and windproof lighters.

Fire can completely change a situation from being cold, wet and unbearable to dry, warm, and manageable. It's important to be smart and safe with your fire, of course. Fires can be seen at night and the smoke can be seen during the day. If you and your family find yourselves in a dangerous situation where your presence is best left unknown, don't advertise your whereabouts via a campfire. If you're bunking in at home and are not in danger from neighbors or predators, a constant fire can be a great mood-booster, not to mention all of its practical uses as well.

General Supplies and Uses

In the area of general supplies, anything that you think you or your family might benefit from can be on this list. I know, that seems a bit too wide open. But really this is your catchall category. These items are not essential to your survival, but they can help. You'll want items such as can openers, reusable plastic dishes, and eating utensils. Toys or books for the kids. Hand-crank radio. Things of that nature.

If you've stocked up seeds for gardening, then it makes sense that you'll want some gardening supplies. A hoe, rake and shovel are a good place to start. And they have multiple uses such as building traps, or using as a weapon against a would-be intruder. A broom and dustpan are also two tools that can help keep your living area cleaner and free of debris. In the event that garbage pick up is suspended, investing in a metal burn barrel is one way idea to eliminate waste.

With you and your family potentially living in an enclosed area, trash is sure to build up and attract bugs, flies, and animals. Include all kinds of bags in your emergency pantry. Garbage bags and grocery bags can be used for trash and freezer bags can be used to help ration food or even keep each family member's personal items separate.

Bug spray, sunscreen, petroleum jelly, lotions, and creams can help protect you from bugs, the sun, and dry skin. Any one of these factors can turn into a rash that can get infected. The idea is to prevent cuts, scrapes, and rashes to prevent infection but some situations cannot be avoided. If that is the case, you will be glad that you will diligent in your medical supplies.

Other items of interest include duct tape, super glue and zip ties. These items are versatile and have multiple functions around the house. Duct tape can aid in sealing up windows and doors. Super glue can help to make repairs to clothes or light items. Zip ties can be used to consolidating equipment or restraining intruders.

Paracord has many uses from hammocks and tents to creating traps for wildlife or a trip wire to alert you of intruders. Paracord can even be intertwined with another rope of paracord to make it stronger and more durable. Many times, the trouble is not with the rope used but with the knot used. Knowing what knot to use and when could save the day. Increase your skill set and knowledge. Pass on the knowledge to your spouse and children. Learn together and grow together.

Lastly, here are a few items that are useful to keep on hand that may be overlooked in your initial planning. Maps of the local area and surrounding larger areas are useful in case you do have to leave your shelter. Writing instruments, pens, pencil, pencil sharpeners, paper, and sharpies can be used to keep young children out of your hair or for writing down your thoughts. Sharpies are always useful for labeling foods, box, and cans. Aluminum foil seems to always have a use, even if it's just cooking by campfire. A spare cell phone that runs on prepaid minutes could be the deciding factor in your situation if you and your family are barricaded in a dangerous zone. If you have any pets, you will want to include extra pet food and extra water for them. Keeping them alive and with you will be an enormous morale booster, so don't forget to plan for Fido. Any comfort foods or sweets that are non-perishable can be included in your pantry. A small treat from time to time can also aid in boosting morale and motivation.

Defense and Security

So, you've built up your pantry and have a whole host of supplies. Excellent. Now comes another problem to address. How do you defend yourself, your family, and your emergency pantry? It is no secret that many people don't really plan for emergency situations beyond a credit card and rushing to the grocery store. Looting and rioting is a real and present danger. The local law enforcement may be so overwhelmed that you are on your own until they arrive. An even scarier situation is that local law enforcement may never arrive. What will you do in that situation?

Some people believe that if they keep to themselves and keep their head down that they will remain unscathed. This is not usually true, as we have seen in the case of a terrorist act (September 11th attacks) or a natural disaster (Hurricane Katrina). People are caught in the crossfire of war and natural disaster everyday. When the aftermath of these events are disorder, people will act as though everyone and everything is fair game. People revert to a more vicious, barbaric state of being when their survival is threatened. Fighting in the grocery stores, fighting in the streets, and people whose goal is to take what you have prepared is a situation that you need to prepare for and it can be deadly for you and your family if you don't.

Some challenges to defense and security are the law and your own code of ethics. The federal law states that defending oneself or others using reasonable force is legal. As a response to an unquestionably unlawful act with reasonable belief that the act will result in fighting with injurious or fatal consequences, defense up to and including deadly force may be used. Some states have a "duty to retreat" clause, with the exceptions that only if the person is unable to safely retreat or they are already in their own home, deadly force may be used. If law enforcement is active when you are presented with a situation or if law and order gets reestablished after your situation is resolved, you may still have to contend with legal fallout. Of course, this will be less important if society has well and truly broken down. In that scenario, it won't matter what the laws and regulations are: you will need to protect your family at all cost.

There are some people who will avoid violence to the extent that it may cost them their life. There are people that believe that negotiating with their attackers can resolve the situation. You have to decide to what extent you are willing to defend yourself, your family, and your preparations. If you perish, will your family be safe? Or will they fall victim to the attackers as well? Most intruders don't stop at "just what they need". If you are willing to do what is necessary to protect and defend you and yours, then you need to prepare your mind and your body. It's not an easy thing to approach, but if you are truly going to be prepared for any situation, it's a vital step along the way.

First things first: raise your awareness. All the guns and self-defense training in the world are useless to you if you are caught unaware.

Should you find yourself in a disaster-type situation, you may have to do tasks that require you to pay attention. And it's easy to get so caught up in completing a task that you forget to look around. A way to train yourself to look around is set an alarm every ten minutes. As you do tasks around the house, when your watch or phone goes off, look up and look around. Eventually, as you're working, you'll find yourself looking periodically and you will notice when time has passed and you haven't looked around. You'll become more aware of your surroundings. You'll notice when something doesn't seem quite right. This can be the difference between survival or not one day, so take the time to practice these skills now.

One way to involve your family, if they are old enough, is to have them take turns as watchers. Teach them what to be aware of such as sounds of movement, moving bushes, concealed people, people who are trying to conceal themselves, suspicious behavior or activity, and groups of people. No matter how trivial, train yourself and your family to watch with their eyes and their ears. At the end of the task or activity, ask what they have seen and why it caught their attention.

Some ways to prepare for to defend yourself and you family is increasing your knowledge in both unarmed self-defense and armed self-defense. You will want to explore non-lethal and lethal methods of defense. Above all, the mindset to take action is important. Know what danger looks like and take action.

Next, look at your defense options. You can increase your knowledge by taking self-defense classes. A few well-learned basic moves trump a bunch of over-elegant half-learned moves. And, anything can be a defense weapon in a survival situation, like a golf club, sturdy walking stick, baseball bat, rock, cane, flashlight, or even a pen.

Non-lethal defense weapons can be weapons such as these:

Batons ($16 online): Batons can give you the advantage of reach.

Stun Guns ($11 online): It temporarily disables your assailant in close encounters due to an electrical shock.

Expandable Stun Baton ($40 online): Gives you the advantage of reach plus the whole baton (minus the handle) stuns. If your assailant tries to grab the baton, they get stunned.

Pepper Spray ($16 online): It temporarily disables your assailant with blinding liquid, pain causing pepper spray.

Pepper Gun ($55 online): Trigger-activated and shoots accurate and continuous stream of   pepper spray up to 25 ft.

Any one of these weapons can be kept in your home for close encounters. For lethal weapons, you might consider investing in a gun. There are several types of guns and if you are considering a gun as a measure of defense or otherwise, there are a few things you need to know. The most common types of guns owned by civilians are pistols, revolvers, shotguns, and rifles.

Pistols are loaded with clips and the clips are loaded with bullets. Revolvers differ from pistols in that the bullets are slid directly into the individual bullet chambers and not slid into a clip, which is then inserted into a gun. An advantage of pistols is that clips hold more bullets than a revolver and you can carry spare clips. An advantage of revolvers is that you don't need a clip to load the gun. You can carry the spare ammo on your person and reload as need. Pistols and revolvers are accurate in long distances (up to a certain range) or close encounters.

A shotgun is smoothbore, meaning that the inside of the barrel has no grooves and is either single-barreled or double-barreled. A single-barrel dispenses one shotgun shell; a double barrel dispenses two shotgun shells, one from each barrel. Shotguns are more accurate in close encounters and not very accurate in long range. They do a considerable amount more damage than a standard pistol or revolver, however.

Rifles have a barrel 16 inches or longer and the inside of the barrel has spiraled, parallel grooves (hence the term, rifle) that spin the bullet as it moves out the barrel upon discharge. This allows for a longer range of accuracy. Rifles can be used for hunting or by a watcher, as can a shotgun. A pistol or revolver can be carried on your person and concealed so as not to draw attention.

Owning a gun in your home can give you and your family a real sense of security. It is a deterrent to would-be intruders and can induce instant compliance. Rifles can be used to hunt wildlife and provide dinner should your disaster situation last longer than your emergency pantry. Guns can be the factor that increases your advantage in a confrontation.

The other side of the coin is that a gun in the home increases the risks of accidents. Even when the gun is securely locked, the possibility that your children will gain access somehow is present. Guns at home are frequently used in suicides and accidental shootings of a family members, neighbors, and friends. Even when you take every precaution imaginable, the unimaginable can happen. This is something you need to discuss with your family and take the proper steps, such as gun safety training, hunting lessons, and proper gun ownership courses.

Other challenges to gun ownership are presented by the law. The federal law prohibits certain people from owning guns such as people with felonies, misdemeanors, or dishonorable discharge from the military. Fugitives, illegal aliens, people diagnosed with mental illness, people who have renounced their U.S. Citizenship, people convicted of a domestic violence misdemeanor, and people subject to particular restraining orders are also on the list prohibiting gun ownership. States may require registration, licenses or permits to own, open carry, conceal carry, or transport. Most all states require background checks for firearm purchases. Some states recognize others states laws and some do not. If you decide that having a gun present is necessary for you and your family, do research on what options meets your and your family's needs. From there, create a safety plan with your family to help lower the risk of a gun-related accident.

You can never plan for every scenario that could happen or go wrong. Should you find yourselves in a survival situation, there are some safety precautions you and your family can take. If you have to go anywhere, don't go ill prepared and never go alone. Have a weapon to defend yourself and someone by your side to double your chances of success. If your family consists of two adults and small children, your decisions are more delicate. Perhaps you can have checkpoints and the other adult can act as a watcher, scanning the area for what you cannot see. At night, don't use any light, candles, or fire. A single candle can be distinguished up to 30 miles away by the human eye. If light is absolutely necessary, keep your curtains closed and your windows boarded up.

By having the knowledge and mindset to defend yourself and your family at any cost, you will have increased your chances of survival but there is one more *very* important concept to understand. That is that you should always try to avoid avoidable situations. You may be armed to the teeth to defend and protect, but each encounter slurps up resources and presents a possibility of injury and infection. If you can achieve your goal without a confrontation, do it. Make the smarter choice and increase your chances of long-term survival.

Securing Your Shelter

Another step in preparing yourself and your family is fortifying your home, also known as your Shelter-In-Place. Outside your home you will want objects that alert you to an outsider's presence. One way to achieve this is to have floodlights or motion sensor strobe lights outside your home. Another way to alert you and your family is to have watchers or a guard dog. Or, you can collect cans, put a few marbles or noisemakers inside and string them low to the ground. You can even have rope pulled taut on the ground tied to the cans in the trees, so when the rope is stepped on, the cans in the trees make noise. If you need to, you can even create pit traps. None of these need to cost much money.

Any easy trap is to dig a deep hole at least 12 feet deep. Cover the hole with a light grid of twigs that will easily snap under pressure. Then, cover the grid with leaves. Of course, you don't want your family or the mailman wandering through that area. It may be better to dig the hole after the disaster strikes.

From inside the house, what you need to focus on securing are the entrances, exits, windows, and vents. While some people go all the way with bars on the windows, some people don't like the idea of getting trapped in their own homes should an intruder get the best of them. A compromise is to have a way to quickly fortify your home at a moment's notice.

For boarding up your windows and doors, you'll want to have enough wood to block all your windows and doors. Cut the wood to fit your windows and doors. Invest in an electric drill (as low as $25); keep it fully charged and next to your pre-cut wood. Screws are favored over nails in this case, should you have to remove the panels and make a getaway. When you install the wood panels, do it on the inside of the house and behind the curtains. There's no need to advertise your presence. Store the wood in the room. Make sure that it's easily accessible.

In case of a biological airborne attack, you'll want to secure every door, window, vent, crack and crevice that could let air from the outside flow inside. To do this, get plastic sheeting ($5 per 10 ft. x 10 ft. online). You'll want plastic thicker than plastic food wrap. Pre-cut the sheeting to fit all your windows and doors in each room because you never know what room you will be in. Pre-cut sheeting for every vent and outlet, and don't forget the vent over your stove. The official rule for breathable air is 10ft x 10ft of space per person to prevent carbon dioxide build up. This is for up to 5 hours. To secure your room, securely duct tape the sheeting over the windows, doors, vents, and outlets and duct tape any cracks. The goal is to prevent any outside air from entering the room. To store your supplies, have a storage unit marked (Shelter-in-place sheeting) and easily accessible. Store your pre-cut plastic sheeting and a couple rolls of duct tape in each room.

Insides defenses could include keeping a club, walking stick, baseball bat, knife or any object that can be used for defense in each room in an easily accessible spot that does not change. A note of interest is operational security. You don't want your preparations and defenses to be public knowledge. Your nice neighbors may have a nastier side in a disaster scenario. Communicating to your family the importance of silence is imperative for the sake of survival. Also, suppose stragglers wander by, posing no threat, seeking a meal and some water. Will you deny them? Will you feed them? There's no way to know if they won't return with a mob to take your food. You have to decide what you can spare, if anything at all. If your emergency pantry is strict in rations, then you have nothing to spare. Not sticking to your preparedness plan is like not having a plan at all.

Plan B

Plan B is to Bug Out. Bugging out means leaving your home or shelter and heading to another home or shelter. This bug out location should be safe, secure, and stocked with a few days worth of food for you and your family until you can get situated. This might be a cousin's house on a farm, your parents' house if they have a basement, or a friend in your prepper network. If you have been building an emergency pantry at your home, the idea of leaving your preparations behind might not be resonating with you at all.

There are a few reasons that might lead you to move into Plan B. If your emergency food pantry has depleted, it's time act. You might think to check abandoned houses or start hunting for food. But what if the houses have already been sacked, are still occupied, and the animals are gone? Other reasons that would lead to bugging out are hostility and environmental danger. Even with the best fortified shelters, it only takes time and consistency to eventually become overwhelmed by attackers. And a top of the line, fortified shelter isn't going to stop a flood, wildfire, hurricane, or another natural disaster. It might withstand one, but only for so long. Obviously, bugging out is not going to be your first action, but if it's going to an action at all, it needs to be planned.

Decide on where your bug out location is going to be. If it's a friend or family member's property, you may want to keep them informed of your possible arrival pending a catastrophe. You and your family might be at different locations when disaster strikes and if none of you can make it to your shelter-in-place due to hazard and road conditions, how do you reconnect? Can your important documents be recovered? Who is going to pick up the kids from school? Before you ever reach that scenario, you need to have predetermined checkpoints and a plan of action in place. Everyone in the family should know their checkpoint and know where they are headed if disaster strikes. You could perhaps station one checkpoint for each side of your town or city. Or you could have different checkpoints for different days of the week. Such as, Mondays and Wednesdays and Fridays are checkpoint 1 and Saturdays, Sundays, Tuesdays, and Thursdays are checkpoint 2.

Now, bugging out is only as good as your route. If your normal exit route takes you and your family back into the fray, then your escape route is compromised. One way to avoid a compromised escape route is to have Alternate Escape Routes.

Alternate escape routes are routes that are basically another way to get where you're going. It helps if they are less commonly used, traffic-jam free and lead out towards your destination. Many times when cities are evacuated, the main roads and normal routes are cluttered with cars and people. Your alternate escape routes will allow you to exit the city and avoid being stuck out in the open, in a crowd of scared, angry citizens, with your family.

If you can, recover your safe box with all your important documents in it. These include birth certificates, driver' licenses, marriage license, gun permits or registrations (if you have one), social security cards and anything else that is important. You may even want to include a few photos for a taste of home.

Involving Your Family

Family can be a hard thing to motivate when it comes to prepping. Transitioning to a lifestyle of preparedness means getting vigilant and prudent and *staying* vigilant and prudent. The change is not always welcome. Some ways to involve your family is to communicate that "the phase" will not pass. Talk with them about the benefits of a preparedness lifestyle. Explore techniques and put them to the test, such as a your gear, skills, and awareness. Make sure they know how to use waterproof matches or magnesium and flint and how to safely build a fire. As you learn, teach them also. Teach them different knots and paracord uses and how to build traps and tarp lean-tos, and how to hunt and garden. Camping is as good a time as any to test your skills. Make it a fun family event to go camping once a month or so. This will help everyone in your family become used to the outdoor, survival lifestyle. After all, you want to know what techniques and gear work well and which ones don't. Waiting until disaster strikes to find out what works is an ill-advised plan.

If you have made a list for the items in your emergency pantry, perhaps let your family loose in the thrift store or flea market. Set them on a hunt for the lowest priced pantry items. One way to really get your family involved is by having them build their own bug out bags. It can be a really fun exercise for children, and it helps them feel invested and responsible for something.

Having your family involved in the evacuation plans, alternate escape routes and checkpoints is another way to have them involved. The more invested they are in the plan from the beginning, the more likely they are to remember the plan because they were a part of building it rather than merely being told what the plan is.

Your family can also be involved in the maintenance of your emergency pantry. As you acquire supplies and food on your list, you will want to check it off the list. You can have someone label the food with the date acquired, the expiration date and the ingredients the day it's brought home. Next, create a separate inventory list of what you have acquired so far. A subject notebook will do. In this notebook will be a Column 1 with the name of the food or supplies. Column 2 will have the date acquired. Column 3 will have the Expiration date.

Write down your entire emergency pantry as you acquire it. This is also a task that a family member can do. For rotation, you can have a family member check the dates in the inventory book weekly and pull all foods or supplies that expire in 1 or 2 months time. You can use these items by rotating them out. As you repurchase these items, rotate them back into your budget and emergency pantry. Label the items and record them in your inventory book. This ensures that your pantry is up-to-date with useable goods and your family isn't wasting any food or money by letting items go bad.

Labeling cans and writing an inventory can get tedious, so mix things up by rotating weekly shifts. These shifts will add responsibility and keep the preparedness lifestyle at the forefront of your family's mind. Continue to stress that scared people are angry people and can become dangerous people. The need for concealing your plans and preparations is imperative as is avoiding avoidable situations.

Prepping on a budget has its challenges, but you and your family can't afford to *not* prepare. Prepping may seem like a lot of work for a never-ending job. Don't let yourself get discouraged before you ever begin. Any preparation, no matter how small is one more advantage you and your family will have. Even when you are ever so slowly moving forward, it is better than standing still, and you and your family will benefit from it. Go steady but go forward.

Closing Thoughts

Once you have prepared for natural disasters and assessed how well your home is protected, then it's time to make sure that you and your family are ready to get where you need to be. Prepping is a lifestyle and a choice that you can make today. It can seem intimidating at first, but the sooner you start, the better off you will be. It doesn't have to break the bank and, if done correctly, it will even help you save a lot of money in the long run. From buying food in bulk, to using coupons, to starting early and saving often, there are many ways to make prepping more affordable and more achievable for any person or family.

You don't need to spend money on every latest gadget and toy, every item marketed as a "must-have" or a "life-saver". There are now entire businesses set up just to try to convince people that they *need* to buy a certain item to survive, or they *just must* subscribe to a monthly service and receive a new survival item every month. Simply not true! People have been prepping for generations without any of those things, and those same prepping principles are still more than useful today.

At its core, prepping is about securing the future of you and your family. So it makes sense that a big part of this equation is to do it all without incurring huge amounts of debts and making yourself beholden to some big bank or credit card company. We need to be prepared not only physically, but mentally and financially as well. We have no way of knowing what events will be coming our way, but it only makes sense to prepare the same, whether it's a natural disaster, a society disaster, or a global financial collapse. If you follow the principles of prepping on a budget, you'll be in the best possible position to deal with whatever comes our way. And really, that's what this is all about!

*****

The Urban Prepper: A City Survival Guide

Prepping. We've all heard of it, but have you ever really thought about what it means? In the broadest sense, prepping is a term that refers primarily to the practice of survivalism in its modern context. While the general idea has been around for centuries, it has not had the same connotation in previous time periods as it does in our modern era. The age of consumerism and relative comfort in which we live has caused many of the survival skills and our general level of preparedness to dwindle down to near nothing, particularly in urban areas. The reasoning for this is simple: with everything either immediately available or just a short email or phone call away, many people believe that there is little or no need to maintain any sort of preparatory inventory or plan in case of disaster. The hard truth of it is, most people just believe that everything will work out regardless of their circumstances and, thus, believe that preparation is not necessary. Unfortunately, that is not the case.

Survivalism is a method of ensuring survival and remaining self-sufficient during times following a catastrophe, disaster, national or international emergency, or political and/or social upheaval. One particular area of interest, which has important implications for millions of city dwellers today, is the art of urban prepping. Urban prepping is different from traditional prepping in a number of key ways and, given the growing number of people residing in urban environments, is of particular importance to even greater numbers of people these days. Without the presence of a large amount of land or the ability to store emergency supplies in a cellar or a similar storage space, there can be some difficulty in urban prepping. These challenges can be overcome, but they require particular attention to detail.

Urban environments are generally defined by two primary characteristics: a higher human population density and a much higher level of human development than the areas that surround it. Urban areas can include towns, cities, and a number of other types of human settlements. The term does not, however, include small human settlements such as villages or hamlets. The areas that surround dense urban environments can quickly become something called "urban sprawl" through a process known as urbanization. Urban sprawl can sometimes include suburban areas. They are typically not as developed as cities, but they do have a relatively high human population and all of the services that come along with that. In the United States, there are two terms that are used to describe urban environments: urbanized areas and urban clusters. Places with a human population of fifty thousand or more are urbanized areas. Urban clusters are urban areas with a population of less than fifty thousand.

Some of the most important aspects of urban prepping are also the factors that differentiate it from traditional prepping. One of these aspects is the creation of a bug-out bag and an evacuation plan. During times of disaster, cities are likely going to become one of the most dangerous environments for people to try and survive in. This is primarily because of the high population, the close quarters, and the lack of natural resources. Should the electricity and/or water utilities disappear, cities would quickly become very dangerous. It is, therefore, pertinent to have a plan, the skills, and the basic equipment on hand at all times in order to move away from these areas in the event of a true survival or disaster situation. The amount of space you have to prepare in an urban setting is far less than you would have if you were residing in even a suburb or out in a rural area. Thus, it is very important to prioritize your preparation.

Preparedness Checklist in Order of Importance

1. Water
2. Emergency Kits
3. Food
4. Other supplies

The Essential First Step: A Bug-Out Bag

A bug out bag is a kit that is portable and easy to carry. It should contain everything that a person would need in order to survive for around seventy-two hours in the event of a disaster or a catastrophe. A good bug out bag will include items that are necessary for three possible scenarios.

Scenario 1 – Evacuation within the city

Evacuation within the city would refer to any evacuation that may take place during which a person must move from their home within the city to another location within the city. This could include things such as moving to a bomb shelter or moving to higher ground in case of flooding.

Scenario 2 – Evacuation outside the city
This type of survival situation will require a person to leave the entire city during an evacuation. This may include nuclear or terrorist attacks, invasions, or large-scale natural disasters such as hurricanes. These kinds of evacuations are relatively uncommon in most cities, but they should be prepared for nonetheless.

Scenario 3 – Search and rescue
Even if a person is not personally wounded or directly affected by a survival situation, it is good to have tools in their bug-out bag in the event that someone else is. This will help in being found and rescued when the time comes.

Urban environments, in particular, present certain challenges that are not present in wilderness environments. With that idea in mind, it is important to remember that the bug-out bag for each of these two types of situations will also be different. The bug-out bag for use in an urban situation is very different from a bug-out bag that may be used in a wilderness situation. The high population and low density of vegetation and wildlife in urban areas can lead to problems that people in rural areas may not encounter. One example of this is a large number of wounded and/or dead such as those found during Hurricane Katrina in New Orleans or during some of the mudslides or tsunami affected areas in Asia.

There are many eventualities that could occur in a survival situation that need to be taken into account when creating a bug-out bag. Dealing with the debris of buildings and glass is an important thing to consider, especially in an urban survival situation. Another thing to consider is the presence of buildings in urban areas. Buildings mean shelter and, thus, it is not as important to consider shelter when building an urban bug-out bag. The chances of encountering other people are high in urban areas and should also be taken into account. You will need to tailor your bug-out bag depending on your specific location and climate.

Essentials of an Urban Bug-Out Bag, apart from Water and Food, which are Critical!

Crowbar – A crowbar is so useful in an urban setting it almost needs no explanation. This can help pry open doors or to move stuck objects. It can be used to smash through problem areas if they are encountered and it also doubles as a melee weapon. If you are preparing bug-out bags for your entire family, one crowbar should be sufficient.

Hydrant/Gas Main Tool – Fire hydrants may be able to provide a source of fresh water if no other water can be found, particularly in urban environments. Gas mains in houses will often need to be shut off in the event a fire must be made or simply for safety reasons. A tool that can be used to open and close both should be included in the bag.

Multitool – There are almost too many uses for a multitool to name. This is an essential addition to any bug-out bag. You'll find it coming in handy in a variety of situations and it's one of those simple items that most people will simply forget to have on hand, so if you pack one in your bug-out bag, you'll be ahead of the curve already.

Map and Compass – Knowing the surrounding area and how to navigate it is essential in a survival situation. Particularly in urban areas, where it can be easy to get lost. Coupled with a good route that has been pre-planned and that every individual in your family knows, this can provide an easy way to safety. Maps should be carried at all times and should be distributed to any immediate members of the family. There are a few different routes that need to be planned out on a map for maximum effectiveness:

Highway route – This should be your best option. Also, the first option that will likely be unusable in the event of a disaster or an emergency.

Back-road route – Should the highways be unavailable, side and back roads are the next best option.

Off-road route – Should all of the other possible routes be inaccessible, an off-road route outside of the city may be the only choice.

Routes to important people – extended family, close family, etc. It is important to have these people on a survival map in order to find them without the need of GPS or other electronic services. They can be important resources in a survival situation.

Rendezvous points – For anyone who may get lost. This is going to be the primary method by which people can meet up in the event that they are separated.

Additional Items to include in your Bug-Out Bag:
Work Gloves – In urban environments, there are many hazards one may have to cross in order to reach safety or even to simply move around. A pair of sturdy work gloves can prevent the hands from being damaged or cut by broken glass, metal, or building materials that may have fallen. This is a simple thing that most people will forget, so having a good pair of work gloves will give you an immediate advantage.

Writing Tool (Chalk, Permanent Marker) – This is being listed as an essential because it is both useful and it is lightweight and compact. A writing tool can be used to leave messages for other survivors or to mark certain areas as dangerous. Good communication has a myriad of benefits, all of which can be attained simply by using a good writing tool.

Can Opener – self-explanatory. A city provides many opportunities to find canned food and canned food is next to useless without a can opener. Having a working can opener can save a person the frustration and potential danger of trying to open a can with another tool (such as a knife).

Mask – In urban areas, the high number of buildings increases the potential for dust and airborne particulates. The high building density also increases the risk of fire. A good mask can prevent the inhalation of particulate matter and can prevent smoke from entering the lungs (at least to a degree).

Metal Spork – The one utensil a person will need. This is a catch-all eating utensil that is good for both "wet" food such as soup and solid food such as meat.

LED Flashlight – The buildings in an urban environment can block sunlight and make the entire area much darker than it would be otherwise. If a person must travel inside buildings or underground for any period of time, you're going to need a good source of light. A solar powered flashlight would be best because it could simply charge outside during the day while traveling. Battery powered flashlights are not a bad thing to have, but one should keep in mind that they do rely on batteries, which adds another item to carry and another thing to worry about running out of.

Hand-Crank Radio – A good radio to pick up signals from other survivors or from emergency personnel is essential. Hand crank, again, is better than battery powered because it doesn't rely on the ability to find batteries to work.

Water Purification Tablets – Another essential. Water purification tablets can work in a pinch if water is not available and if boiling is not an option. Carry enough for around 72 hours, per person.

Flint and Steel – Flint and steel are essential for any survival situation in order to start a solid fire.

Small Mirror – Lightweight. Portable. Mirrors can help signal others, to help direct and focus sunlight in order to start fires, and to check around corners and other hard to see areas for protection.

Medications – In addition to any essential personal medication, it is good to carry Neosporin, aspirin, and a small bottle of alcohol or peroxide for cleaning wounds.

Antibiotics are a form of medication that is often overlooked by the prepping community as a whole. The reasoning is that they either do not understand what to buy, do not understand the proper storage, or do not believe that antibiotics are something that can simply be obtained easily enough to make them viable. Urban preppers have a benefit insofar as they have access to many more resources than preppers in rural or wilderness areas. Animal antibiotics can be used in humans as well, since they are inherently the same chemicals. It should be noted that antibiotics inherently treat bacterial infections. They are useless in the case of viral infections such as colds or flu.

Amoxycillin – sold as Fish-Mox at most pet stores. Amoxycillin is a powerful antibiotic that can be used to handle bacteria, which cause middle ear and/or respiratory infections. It is also safe for pregnant women and children. There is a possibility for allergy, however, so care should be taken.

Ampicillin – sold as Fish-Cillin in many pet stores. Useful for urinary tract infections, gastrointestinal problems, respiratory problems, or the myriad of things that penicillin is useful for. Less likely to cause allergic reactions than penicillin or amoxicillin.

Metronidazole – sold as Fish-Zole. This is useful for diabetic foot ulcers, gastrointestinal problems, joint and bone infections, meningitis, and many other types of bacterial infections.

Food – Canned food can be good, but it is extremely bulky. It is better to pack high protein and high calorie meals, if possible. Energy bars make a good choice, as do things like beef jerky. Pack enough canned food for at least 72 hours, per person, if possible.

Cooking items: Make sure to have a small backpacking stove and fuel, in addition to a small pot or a large cup for boiling water and cooking food.

Waterproof Matches – Another backup. Just in case fire cannot be started with the flint and steal, a small container of waterproof matches can work as a backup.

In addition to the essentials, there are a number of pieces of accessory equipment that can be included in a bug-out bag. Weight is always a factor in a survival situation and should be kept in mind when deciding what sorts of accessory equipment to include.

Accessory Equipment for an Urban Bug-Out Bag
Clothing – Clothing is being listed under accessory supplies for two reasons: It is heavy and it is bulky. Wear what you need, and maybe have an extra outfit ready to go if you need it. Don't pack a lot of clothes, however. If you pack anything, pack extra socks and underwear.

Rain Gear – Rain gear is a certain subset of clothing that includes ponchos and waterproof gear that can be useful during times of rain. This gear is useful but will not necessarily be essential in an urban environment because of the presence of so many buildings. It is very likely that a person could find an area to shelter themselves from the rain relatively easily.

Money – Money may or may not be useful. It might be nice to have in some situations, since the ATMs probably will not be working during a survival situation, but it may not be useful the longer the survival situation drags on. A person has to assume that money wouldn't be as useful in huge disaster situations so it may not be needed. During short-term survival situations, it is also hard to think of a reason to need money. Who will take the money? This is a toss-up – take some if you think it will be helpful, but don't worry about stocking up on huge piles of cash.

Tarp – Tarps are heavy and they are bulky. You must weigh the pros and cons when deciding whether to include them in your bug-out bag. They can be used as makeshift shelters, to help carry items, or to protect a group from the elements.

Paracord – Paracord has a myriad of uses. One of the best uses it to either tie things for dragging (such as a sled on which supplies or injured persons can be placed). Another use, though not quite as important in an urban environment, is its ability to hold up tarps or other coverings and to work as the backbone of makeshift shelters.

Batteries – Batteries are not as important as the essential items for two reasons: in an urban environment, they will probably be relatively easy to find and most of the items in the bug-out bag should be self-sufficient (solar flashlights, hand crank radio, flint and steel, etc).

One important thing to note about bug-out bags is that they are not the only things that a person will need to survive. Just as important, if not more than, as the bug-out bag itself is the knowledge that a person brings to the table. Knowledge truly is power and one of the best ways to prepare for any type of disaster is to have basic knowledge of survival and environmental conditions. Even the best laid plans and the best bug-out bag cannot prepare you for every scenario, so it is important to have knowledge to back up your tools and equipment. It is important to know where things are in relation to each other in your area, the safe methods and areas of travel, where one might find help should they need it, and the general flora and fauna that can be found in the area. This sort of knowledge can provide a lot of help should a person need to modify their plans while on the move.

Another thing to keep in mind is that a person should carry certain essential items (such as flint and steel) in their survival bag regardless of their location. Even in an urban environment, where it doesn't seem like a good idea to make a fire, a person can never know when it may be necessary. There is always the possibility of migrating out of the initial urban environment toward more rural areas as well.

Home Preparations

Even in an urban survival situation, having your home prepared for moderate to long-term survival is a good idea. It pays to be prepared for any situation. With that in mind, there are a number of things an urban prepper can have around which will help greatly, depending on their exact living situation. Most of these items are large and are not meant to be carried anywhere, but rather kept within the home for the duration of the situation. Should a person need to leave, very few of them will even be a viable option for carrying.

Generator – Electricity will probably be one of the first things to go in a survival situation. A small generator can keep the juice flowing long enough to settle any last minute issues.

Gasoline – At least ten gallons would be best. Gasoline may be at a premium during a survival situation, but this amount will keep things moving long enough to get settled. Make sure you have it stocked, because at the first sign of disaster, the gas stations will fill with long lines of unprepared people who are looking to fill their tanks. You want to avoid that situation and so should have a small stock of gasoline on your premises at all times.

Chainsaw – Preferably gas powered. Chainsaws are useful for hundreds of things, but in an urban situation there may be a need to move through fallen debris or to cut a new way out of an area.

Heavy tools – An axe, a sledgehammer, and a large tool kit (at minimum). This is important for both moving through the environment, clearing areas near the home that may be blocked or inaccessible, and taking apart or repairing the myriad of items a person may find within the urban environment.

Beyond preparing items in the home, there are a few security issues that a prepper may want to take care of as well. Urban preparation in this regard is almost nothing like rural prepping. There will be no bunkers or fences to put up in an urban area. Instead, preppers must simply work with what they have got. That means fortifying doors and windows, among other things. A heavy steel door should be a priority, if possible. Windows can be reinforced with locks and steel mesh, if necessary.

One important thing to remember: an urban home only needs to be prepared for the length of time a prepper plans to spend in it. If the plan during the survival situation is to leave the home immediately and try and find a safe place or to migrate out of the city, then there is no need to put extra reinforcement into the home or to keep long term supplies there. If you are planning to bunker down in your condo or urban home for an extended period of time, you're going to want to reinforce your home as highly as possible. It all depends on the exact plans of each individual prepper.

Health, Nutrition, and Fitness

Health, nutrition, and fitness play an enormous role in any survival situation. In urban survival situations, however, they play a larger than normal role. Physical fitness is something that preppers can look to that will greatly increase their chance of survival. A prepper should work on being physically fit prior to any event occurring and should train for the general environment that they may find themselves in. For urban populations, that means preparing for survival within an urban environment. Food and water are always priorities. Preparations for urban survival should include both a knowledge of where to find food and water in addition to storage of food and water within the urban dwelling. Finally, it is important to have a good knowledge of the various hazards that may present themselves during an urban survival situation.

Any given survival situation will only go as smoothly as the health of the survivor allows. It is important to stay healthy and physically fit in order to be prepared for any possible eventualities that could occur. A proper physical fitness routine for a wilderness area may include basic weight exercises, cardiovascular exercise, and endurance exercises. The type of preparation a person should do for urban survival should lean more toward endurance and weight training than cardiovascular work. Staying moving in a city can prove difficult given the high probability of obstacles (cars and trucks, damaged buildings, etc). Movement may not be as quick but it will be more physically taxing.

One type of exercise, in particular, that may be useful in urban areas is parkour. Parkour is a cross-disciplinary type of exercise that emphasizes freedom of movement through environments (particularly urban environments). With a bit of training ahead of time, many obstacles that seem like they cannot be overcome will seem like child's play. Particularly when it comes to traversing ledges, through tight spaces, and maneuvering around obstacles. It is very likely, in an urban survival situation, that cars, trucks, and other debris will be present and will block many potential routes through the environment. With parkour training, the mind will quickly be able to find ways to overcome these various obstacles. Most parkour training will focus on climbing obstacles and jumping between them. Landings are also an important focus. Landings and rolls are of interest to practitioners of parkour because they can reduce the damage and stress on the body that is caused by falling or jumping an appreciable distance.

As with rural prepping situations, food is still a good thing to store in the home. There is a chance that, even in an urban environment, people will either be asked to remain within their homes or their home will prove to be the safest place to be. If that is the case, stored food will be a lifesaver. The priority in an urban home will tend to be toward compact and high calorie foods that will not spoil. A shelving unit within a closet or a pantry would suit the urban prepper just fine in terms of storage space. Urban prepping is, at heart, a relatively short-term endeavor. If long-term survival is the goal, leaving the urban environment should become the first priority. For time frames of a month or less, however, the home may be a viable survival space.

The best foods to store in an urban storage are going to be canned and jarred foods. High calorie and high fat and protein foods are the best foods to store. When consumed fat will, contrary to popular belief, stave off hunger. Eating fat is what signals the body to start using its fat reserves for energy and to stop being hungry. Some of the best protein and fat sources to store are canned tuna, chicken, salmon, and other fish (such as sardines). Potted meat and Vienna sausage are also good choices. Vegetables are, also contrary to popular belief, not the best types of foods to store for a survival situation. There is a very simple reason for this: they are low calorie and they take up a lot of space. Some vegetables are good to store, such as large containers of green beans or yams, but for the most part the space requirement that they bring to the table trumps the caloric payoff that they offer. It may also be useful to store lemon juice and salt. Both are capable of helping electrolyte restoration and to help with any number of medical or survival needs. There is, always, the chance of scurvy setting in if enough citric acid is not obtained in the diet. Lemon juice can help prevent this eventuality and has a very long shelf life (the acidity prevents the growth of bacteria).

Salt carries a particular amount of importance in a survival situation. It can be used to store meat long term (through the process of dehydration), it can be used to help fight against infections in the throat (gargling with warm salt water), it can be used to cook food (obviously), it can be used to melt ice, it can be used to prevent bugs (putting salt in a doorway will help create a barrier), and it can be used to help relieve the itching that is often associated with bug bites. Salt is easily stored and is one of the most useful things that can be stored in the home.

Beyond canned foods, high calorie carbohydrate sources are a good choice to store for energy purposes. They may not have the nutritional value necessary to sustain long-term survival, but they may be necessary at times in order to maintain energy levels.

Here are a few good choices for calorie dense carbohydrates to prep:

White rice – a single cup of white rice can contain over two hundred calories. Given that most stores carry bulk bags (up to fifty pounds) of rice it is possible to get a couple of bags and have enough food to last for months.

Dried beans – beans are sold in bulk and only need to be rehydrated for use in cooking applications. As a source of protein and carbohydrates, beans are a calorie dense food that does not take up a lot of space and can be stored in the home.

Sugar

Powdered drink mix – high in calories in addition to having a ton of vitamins and minerals.

Food that can be taken on the go should be able to last, at minimum, 72 hours. Beyond that, it is going to be up to the survivor to find more food. The best choices are going to, again, be high fat and high protein sources. Carbohydrates, at least as far as canned foods go, are not good choices to bring because of the weight and space requirement. Canned tuna and canned chicken breast are great choices as far as protein sources go. For carbs on the road, it is best to pack some sort of high calorie and high sugar candy. This can keep the survivor moving on the road throughout the day, help to stave off hunger, and has a low space and weight requirement.

Urban environments do not completely remove the capability of preppers to garden. A good seed stock should be kept in the home and can be rotated every couple of years as the viability of the seed stock drops. Though the land area is often much lower in urban environments than it is in rural areas, small gardens can still be created in yards. Hydroponic grow setups can be created in cities. The issue with hydroponics during survival situations, however, is that electricity and water is required to keep them running. This is not even taking into account the need for fresh nutrient solutions, which will not be available if a disaster occurs.

As a way to recap this section, here's a handy guide to help you stock up on food prepping in an urban environment.

10 Best Survival Foods at Your Grocery Store

This most recent winter taught all of us that disasters and emergencies can strike without warning. It also showed us the importance of being prepared. Buying provisions like food and water during or right before a disaster is typically not an option because most stores stock less than a week's worth of food under normal circumstances and are therefore picked bare during emergencies. Keeping a healthy stock of survival foods on hand is a good way to ensure you and your family weather unexpected emergencies.

Creating a supply of emergency food is as easy as making a trip to the grocery store. Below are ten great survival foods that you can find at your local store. These foods have a long shelf-life (from 2 to 10 years), are calorie dense, and relatively inexpensive. All of these things make these ten foods good choices to keep on hand in the event of a crisis.

Dry Beans: Beans are a super food. They are high in protein and fiber and other nutrients that can help keep you healthy during an extended crisis. They are also an excellent way to feed more than one person as 1 cup of dry beans makes 3 cups of cooked beans. Make it a habit to pick up one or two large bags of beans every time you go to the store. Practically all variety of beans are nutritious and long lasting so feel free to pick your favorite.

Lard: During an emergency situation, you'll need oil for cooking. Lard is long-lasting and high in calories (calories are important during a disaster). Plus, it will add a bit of flavor to your food, which can be hard to come by during a crisis. A little lard goes a long way so one large can will be enough.

Rice: You need carbohydrates to fuel you through a disaster and rice is a cheap and healthy way to keep carbs in your diet. Half a cup of dried rice makes 1 cup of cooked rice so it is also a good way to stretch your food supply. Every time you go to the grocery store, pick up a large bag of rice to add to your emergency food supply.

Canned Meat: Stock up on cans of tuna, ham, and chicken as a great source of protein.

Pasta: Like rice, pasta is a great way to get carbohydrates. Plus, pasta can be very cheap so it is worth stocking up on.

Salt: Every time you go to the grocery story, buy salt. Not only will you use it to help store your emergency food supply, it will also come in handy as a seasoning during a crisis.

Cornmeal: Cornmeal is better to keep on hand than flour because it takes fewer ingredients to make breads with cornmeal than with flour. Just add some lard and salt to cornmeal to make a tasty skillet cake. Additionally, cornmeal has a longer shelf life than flour. It is a good idea to stock up with several 5lb bags of cornmeal.

Canned Fruit and Vegetables: Canned fruit and vegetables don't offer much in the way of calories but they are a good way to keep vegetables and fruits in your diet during an emergency, which is important. Stick with cans of green vegetables and low-acidic fruits like pears because those canned foods have a longer shelf life.

Peanut Butter: Peanut butter is a tasty source of protein and much needed fat. Plus, you'll be happy to have this quick snack on hand during an emergency. Peanut butter can get expensive but if stored properly, it will last for five years so stock up on it every chance you get.

Sugar and Honey: These two sweeteners will store for years (forever, really) and are a good way to add flavor to your emergency food. Add sugar to your rice to create a sweet breakfast cereal.

Placing food in long-term storage requires some preparation. First, it is important to find a cool, dry place that is dark. A basement or cellar is ideal. Try to avoid placing emergency food in the garage because the temperature fluctuates too much and that can affect your emergency food supply.

The best way to keep your food fresh for years is to place it in heavy-duty food-grade sealable containers. Keep your food separated—use one container for beans, one for rice. If you like, you can store the canned foods in sealable containers as well. Doing so will allow you to keep them in one place and make them easy to move if that become necessary. Add salt to the sealable containers (1 cup of salt per 5 gallons of storage space). Put your food into the container, and then place some dry ice on top of your food. The dry ice is key, as it will absorb any oxygen in the container. There are such things as oxygen absorbers but dry ice has the added benefit of being a fumigant, meaning it will kill any bugs that happen to find their way in your food supply. Plus, dry ice is fairly cheap at about $5 or $6 for 5lbs of dry ice. A little bit of dry ice goes a long way; you only need around 1 ounce for 5 gallons of storage area. Because the dry ice is there to preserve your food, it is better to use too much rather than too little so feel free to add 2 ounces of dry ice to your food container as it will not harm the food you are storing. Once you have the salt, food, and dry ice packed in the container, seal it tightly. Put a label on the container that list the ingredients and the date the container was packed.

If you make a point of picking up a couple of these survival food items each time you go to the store, you will quickly have a healthy supply of provisions that will see you and your family through any crisis.

Water

Every prepper knows that water is the most important thing a person can have in terms of survival preparation. The body loses water constantly through exertion. Sweat, urine, and even breath causes water loss. Above average or extreme heat can cause the human body to lose half a gallon or more of water per day. It is important, therefor, to make an effort to drink at least a gallon of water per day. There are a few things that every prepper should keep in their home to help maintain hydration during a survival situation. First and foremost: Stored bottled water. The exact amount is going to depend on the amount of space available, but it is good to keep in mind that the average person needs to drink around a gallon of water a day just to maintain hydration. Beyond stored bottled water, a supply of water purification tablets should be kept along with some lightweight carbon filters. This will both purify the water and allow particulate filtration.

Water on the go is a more difficult matter to handle. Carrying a small stove, carbon filters, and pot in the urban bug-out bag can provide an infinite source of clean water provided boiling is an option. A pack of water filtration tablets can be used to purify and, when used in conjunction with the carbon filters, can purify potentially dirty water sources on the go. It is not recommended to carry more than a canteen (possible gallon sized, if possible) of water at a time due to weight and space requirements. Too much equipment can weigh a person down and make travel more difficult. This issue is of particular importance in urban environments where there is a high potential for debris or other obstacles to block movement, requiring climbing. The average human in good physical condition and good environmental conditions can survive a maximum of around four days without water.

Physical hazards are almost definitely going to be an issue in an urban survival situation and the urban prepper should be aware of and prepare to encounter them during their survival preparations. Some of the primary physical hazards that may be encountered can be downed (live) electrical lines, large pools of water, or fallen buildings. Also be on the lookout for fires, falling debris, and wreckage in the streets. Remember: cities are composed almost entirely of concrete, steel, and glass. When a disaster happens in an urban environment, these three things all become huge obstacles that must be overcome. Preparing for physical hazards can be, first and foremost, a matter of knowing what to expect. Cars will likely be jamming the streets, building debris and glass may be on the streets. If there are fires going on somewhere close, there may be ash or coals on the streets as well. In any event, expect the unexpected. In an ideal situation, the urban prepper will have an outfit ready to go that will take into account all of the physical environmental hazards that may be encountered. A pair of good steel-toed boots, a pair of sturdy cargo pants, a nice and thick cotton undershirt, and a good leather jacket are all good choices. Steel-toed boots can prevent damage to the feet from debris underfoot or from damage from falling objects.

Biological, chemical, or radioactive hazards are something that should be taken into account but are very difficult to prepare for. Hazards can vary drastically depending on the nature of the disaster that befalls the urban environment a prepper finds himself in. During any sort of radioactive event such as a reactor meltdown or a nuclear attack, a city can be either a saving grace or a deathtrap. Radiation tends to absorb into concrete and rebar which will then continue to emit radiation. The first step is to get as far away from the blast area as possible. Remaining upwind of the radioactive event to avoid fallout is of utmost importance

Biological hazards are not as much of an issue in urban environments initially. They pose a larger threat as time goes on. Medical waste and garbage become breeding grounds for disease and bacteria, which can pose a real threat to survivors. Avoid areas that may contain either garbage or medical waste if possible. Rotten food can become a breeding ground for insects and disease as well. Route planning should avoid these areas for two reasons: the potential for disease and the potential for running into other survivors. Survivors may be the biggest threat to overall safety in an urban survival situation simply because of their unpredictability. Careful preparation ahead of time and careful route planning will completely remove any need to go near supermarket type areas for food during a survival situation regardless. Regardless, it may not be possible to avoid all possible biological hazards, especially if foraging becomes a necessity. If that is the case, there are a few hazards that a person should be aware of in urban survival situations.

Specific biological hazards to be aware of:

Insects (bedbugs, roaches, lice, etc.) - These insects will spread very quickly in an urban disaster situation. The primary reason stemming from the fact that no people are bothering to keep their numbers in check anymore. Keeping a bit of diatomaceous earth around to spread at entrances to your home or sleeping environment can go a long way to preventing them from entering your domicile and killing off any insects that have already moved in.

Botulism – Botulism is a potentially fatal illness that is caused by the botulinum toxin that is produced by the bacteria *Chlostridium botulinum*. Spores, which can lead to its production, can be found in soil and water sources. They are typically activated by certain environmental conditions such as certain temperature ranges or low oxygen levels. Food sources can be contaminated by *Clostridium botulinum*. It is important to, especially with canned food and preserved food, cook it thoroughly. If a can seems to be "bulging" at the ends, it is probably contaminated and should not be eaten. Symptoms of infection include becoming tired, weak chest or arm muscles, drooping eyelids, and trouble speaking.

Another possible source of botulism is wound infection. Since *Chlostridium botulinum* can live in soil any open wound can potentially become infected and the situation can quickly become life threatening. It is important to maintain proper wound care and cleanliness in situations when wounds may become exposed.

Mold – Urban environments are often the same types of environments in which mold and mildews thrive. Mold often grows in dark and damp areas. Without electricity and with possible deterioration of urban areas, the entire environment can become a large dark and damp area. Mold can quickly spread via spores. There are a few ways that mold can affect the health of an urban prepper. High numbers of spores within the air can lead to allergy problems (runny nose, possible lethargy, low energy, puffy and red eyes) or asthma problems. There is also the potential for mycotoxins within the spores, which can lead to neurological problems and, potentially, death.

Local threats – Beyond the general threats that can be present in urban areas, it is important to know the threats that are more localized. In the northeast, there will be issues that are not present in the Midwest. One of the most important things a prepper can do is to learn about the potential local threats prior to any sort of survival situation.

Some of the biological hazards that are present in either rural or wilderness areas are not as large a problem in cities, but they could become one as the disaster or survival situation lengthens in time. Wild animals (or even hungry domestic animals) could be loose within the city. In addition, insects such as ticks or mosquitoes could potentially transmit infections to survivors within the urban environment. Mosquitoes, in particular, could become a problem very quickly considering their choice for breeding areas. Mosquitoes typically breed within stagnant pools of water. Even a light rain could provide mosquitoes with an entire slew of new breeding grounds within a city, especially if damage allows water to get into buildings. A person may not think that "wildlife" such as animals, birds (and bird droppings), or biting insects (such as ticks) would become a large issue during an urban survival situation. Everything becomes an issue, however, when a duration of time without regular maintenance by humans allows that to occur.

Chemical hazards are extremely varied. In urban environments especially, it is very important to be mindful of the thousands of chemicals all around. Any water or food source could be contaminated with any number of volatile or toxic chemicals. Without a functioning infrastructure, there is very little to keep water and food sources clean and sterile enough for human consumption. Chlorine and fluorine are regularly added to municipal water supplies in order to kill parasites and bacteria. Without the addition of these chemicals there is nothing stopping water lines from becoming overrun with bacteria. For this reason, it is important to keep food, health supplies, and water prepared in the home in order to last as long as possible without having to forage for food or to find a clean water source. If all else fails, make a backup plan to migrate from the urban environment if the situation seems like it is becoming long-term. One type of chemical hazard to be very aware of is gas. Gas mains could break and leak flammable or deadly gas into urban areas. Beyond that, carbon monoxide is still an issue within cities. If there is a large electrical problem in the city, ozone buildup could also become an issue.

Family Matters: Getting Everyone Involved

The family unit serves a very important purpose in life itself. In a survival situation, family may be the only source of support a person can look to and depend on. One of the major issues in an urban survival situation is that, though the prepper is prepared for survival, the rest of the family may not have the same training or knowledge at their disposal in order to be of much use. It is, therefore, very important to include the family in any survival plans and to make sure that they are well aware of what plans and tools have been set in place for the situation at hand.

The close family unit, the spouse and the children, should be made aware of the survival plan, the preparations in the home, and the possible routes out of the city. There should be a plan in place for what to do in the event of an emergency. At the very least, a specified area to meet should the family be split up at the time of the event should be designated. Perhaps a backup area should be designated as well, just in case. Everyone in the family should be assigned certain tasks and the work should be divided equally if at all possible. The close family can be included in the initial preparations and should be taught any of the relevant skills (fire starting, how to use weaponry, etc).

Extended family is an entirely different subject. If any extended family lives in the immediate area, it may be pertinent to include them in your plans and map out relevant routes between homes. If necessary, either they may need to relocate to the prepared home or the prepper may need to relocate to their home. Either way there is safety in numbers and trustworthy individuals may come at a premium.

Self-Defense in Urban Areas
Self-defense is an aspect of survival that is often overblown in terms of preparation. It is, of course, important. But a person must remember that food, water, and shelter will always come first in a survival situation. In an urban environment, however, there is a much higher chance of encountering another person during any sort

of survival situation. Any interaction with another person without the constraints of normal law and order can deteriorate into a dangerous situation at a moments notice. The exact preparations will, again, depend entirely on the plans that a prepper has made during their route planning and survival planning.

At the most basic level, a prepper should learn at least one form of martial arts. Some are better than others. For hand-to-hand combat, either boxing or grappling skills will serve a survivor well. Particularly in the close quarter areas that urban areas consist of. In addition to basic martial arts training, it may serve a prepper well to study ways of disarming melee weapons or handguns from potential threats. As always, risks should be avoided. With that being said, it can never hurt to expect the best and prepare for the worst.

The most useful piece of non-ballistic weaponry (melee weaponry) to carry will be some sort of hatchet. It is lightweight, provides a myriad of uses, and is not bulky. In addition to a hatchet, it is extremely useful to carry a hunting knife. A person never knows when a knife will be necessary until it is too late and, given the environmental concerns in urban areas, it may become necessary to cut or saw synthetic materials that simple pocket knives are incapable of cutting.

Ballistic weaponry is typically where preppers end up going a bit overboard. Yes, having weapons is an important part of prepping.

But the likelihood of needing fifty thousand rounds of ammunition or an entire arsenal of guns is a bit ridiculous. Defense of the home and the surrounding area should be of primary concern to urban preppers. The high population makes it much more likely that a person may suffer from marauders or attack from other groups of survivors. It pays dividends to prepare for this eventuality regardless of the likelihood of it actually occurring. There are four primary types of weapons recommended to include in an urban home. Pistols, rifles, shotguns, and air powered pellet guns. The best pistol, rifle, and shotgun will depend on the abilities and preferences of each individual prepper. One of each will be fine. Air powered pellet guns are recommended for a few reasons: they are good for small game, the ammunition is extremely cheap, the ammunition is plentiful, and they are powered by air.

If a person has to leave their home, carrying two primary weapons will have the best result, as far as weight and practicality goes. Shotguns may not be a practical weapon to carry around, though given the tight spaces in an urban setting they may be more useful than they would in rural areas. A pistol and a rifle should be sufficient. Beyond that, not much should be needed. A person does not need to be a walking arsenal to be successful in an urban survival situation. If a time comes that someone needs more firepower than a pistol and a rifle, the time has come to find an alternate way out of the situation. Beyond the lack of need, there are space and weight considerations that need to be taken into account. Given all of the equipment a survivor may be carrying and the unique problems associated with navigating through a debris filled urban environment, there is simply no viable reason to add the extra weight that more weapons would allow. Not to mention the added need of carrying another form of ammunition.

As much ammunition can be stored in the home as space allows. Again, it is good to have one of each type of weapon and, obviously, ammunition should only be stored for those weapons specifically. Cleaning kits may also be stored, just in case. A primary concern is often how much ammunition a person should store in their home. The response is: enough. There is really no way to tell. A few boxes of each type of ammunition should be sufficient. If space and money allows, more ammunition will always be a boon to the survival effort. Urban environments may necessitate even more ammunition storage in the home simply because the higher population can allow for many more threats requiring the use of firearms. When moving, however, a couple of boxes of each type of ammunition a person requires will be all that space and weight allow. Ammunition, like it or not, can be bulky. With that being said, it can also be valuable, particularly if it is needed and the situation makes it impossible to find more.

Threat assessment consists of three basic steps: identify, assess, and manage. The identification of potential personal threats will usually come in the form of gut feelings. If an individual, an animal, or a group is seen that just feels off, it may be best to simply avoid them. It is always best to minimize risk. This may mean hiding or taking an alternate route. The primary goal, remember, is survival and rescue. Assessment can be as simple as determining the chances of survival against the potential threat. If alone and facing down a gang or a group that looks dangerous, avoid them at all costs. A firefight should only be considered as a last resort. At no time should a survivor attempt pro-active attack. There is nothing to gain and everything to lose. Survival is, first and foremost, a defensive game. Threat management is simple. Get to a location away from the threat and either move on or wait for the threat to pass. Again, even with weapons and ammunition, it is always going to be a better idea to run than to fight.

It is important to note that, if a person is walking around an urban area with a ton of weapons and firepower, they will immediately be perceived as a potential threat by anyone that they meet. It may be prudent to plan your self-defense accordingly. Especially since urban populations often have a very different outlook on weapons than rural populations do. Any law enforcement or military presence during the survival situation will also, in all likelihood, be less than thrilled to find armed citizens wandering the streets. Carrying as little weaponry as possible is a good rule to go by in an urban area.

A few last minute defense tips all fall under the general heading of: "don't attract attention to yourself unless necessary." Avoid cooking with a lot of spices or fragrant foods that may attract desperate people who are hungry. If possible, simply eat things out of a can or out of a box that does not need to be cooked at all. Fires and food will almost certainly attract attention and not all attention is the kind a person would want to attract.

Protecting Your Apartment or Condo in a Survival Situation
Trying to defend your apartment or condo requires a slightly different approach than protecting your house out in the country or where you may have a bit more land to work with.

The first thing to do is get together several supplies that you will use to fortify and defend your apartment. You will want a few tools: power drill and screwdrivers, hammers, bolt cutters, wood screws and nails. You will also need several 2x4s, chain link fence, bubble wrap and thermal curtains (the kind that block cold, heat, and sunlight). You will also want battery operated door alarms and motion sensors. Because you are preparing for a very dangerous situation, you will also want a way to defend yourself from looters and other anarchist. The best way to do this is with a gun.

Guns
Any gun expert will tell you that handguns require repeated, frequent training in order to be a useful tool for defense. Pulling a trigger is a shocking thing to do and you don't want your first time (or your first time in a while) to be in the middle of a dangerous situation.

Additionally, as well as knowing how to load and unload a handgun, you have to know what to do if the gun jams and you also have to be a decent enough shot to hit a moving target while being terrified and in fear of your life. Despite what movies portray, defending yourself with a handgun can be hard and requires practice.

When someone doesn't have a strong familiarity with guns, a shotgun can be a better choice than a handgun. Shotguns are less likely to jam, and the cocking sound of a shotgun is typically an immediate deterrent to someone who means you ill. It is true that shotguns pack a kick, but if you keep it pressed firmly against your shoulder, your body will be able to absorb most of the kick, making it less powerful. Another positive about shotguns for people not familiar with guns is that buckshot scatters on impact so you do not have to be as good a shot as you do with a handgun. If you miss your target but hit a nearby lamp or table, it is likely the person attacking you will still be struck by buckshot.

How to Fortify Your Apartment
Now that you have your supplies out, the first thing you need to do is fortify your doors and windows. No matter what floor you live on, windows are an entry point to your apartment. Place bubble wrap over your windows to distort the view from the outside into your apartment. It is important to obscure the view of your apartment because looters will be looking for signs of life, and they will assume that if someone is living in the apartment, that person has

provisions. Next, nail panels of chain link fence to your windows so looters can't enter if your windows get broken. It is also a good idea to fence in your patio or balcony as well. Finally, hang the thermal curtains. At night, always keep the curtains completely closed so no one can see inside. Thermal curtains will also keep any light you have on in the apartment invisible to the outside.

The best type of door for your security is a metal fire door but most buildings won't allow you to install one as a front door. During a dangerous situation, the second best option is to reinforce the door you have. In reality, most people trying to enter your apartment by force do so by breaking the doorjamb (not the door). Typically, doorjambs are weak and held together with a few small screws. If you know how, reinforce the doorjamb, hinges, and strike plate with long wood screws.

If you are not sure how to do this, there are many videos and articles online explaining how to best approach the subject. Reinforcing these areas is actually pretty simple but takes time: To reinforce the jamb, just remove the doorstop and replace all the screws with wood screws that will drill into the stud, then pop the doorstop back on. Do the same thing with the screws in the hinges and strike plate, making sure all the new screws drill into the stud. Disaster situation aside, it is actually a very good idea to reinforce these areas anyway since kicking in the doorjamb is usually how burglars get into homes.

Once you've reinforced your doorjamb, place some 2x4s horizontally across your door. Place them several feet apart, one above the doorknob and one below it. Use a drill to secure the boards with heavy screws. If at all possible, make sure some of the screws drill into the studs around your door. Don't place wood vertically or diagonally across the door, as this won't really do anything except waste wood. Once you've put up the 2x4s, fill any cracks or spaces around the door with cloth so no light shows through the door. One of your best lines of defense during a survival situation like this is to make it seem like no one is in the apartment; this means covering up signs of life like light and sound. Looters are less likely to enter your apartment if they think it is empty because they will assume there are no supplies inside.

For additional security, hang a door alarm on the doorknob and place motion detectors in your apartment's high traffic areas. These alarms will not deter a looter but they will give you warning so you have enough time to prepare to defend yourself or escape.

Following these steps and having a decent supply of food and water on hand will help you survive any dangerous emergency situation.

Essential Techniques for Survival

There are certain techniques that will prove useful in any survival situation. Whether in an urban area, a rural area, or a wilderness area, there is some knowledge that is invaluable to possess. Any good prepper will prepare themselves with this knowledge in order to be a more viable survivor. Above all, the most important item that a prepper has is right on top of their shoulders: their brain. Don't panic, stay calm. One of the key aspects of prepping is to have a plan and knowledge in place to prevent panic during a survival situation. It will pay dividends for any urban prepper to not only gain the knowledge of these survival techniques, but to actually attempt them at some point. Knowledge can only go so far without real experience.

Fire starting – Fire is the single most important skill a person can have. In urban populations, many people have never even set a fire by themselves. Electricity and amenities like clean running water and air conditioning have prevented the population from needing to know techniques such as building and maintaining a fire. Typically, people will assume that there is no reason to have a fire in an urban area. This is not the case. Some areas are either cold year round or get cold during certain seasons. Either way, if a survivor must remain in the environment for one reason or another, it is very important to know how to stay warm. Fires can, aside from simply heating an area, be used to purify water, cook food, or as a signal.

Where to build: Building fires in urban areas can be a problem for a number of reasons. Building inside can potentially result in buildings catching fire and starting an even bigger problem. Building outside can attract people who could, potentially, be dangerous. The primary reason for not wanting to attract people is this: by the time a fire is needed in an urban environment, it is safe to assume that rescue efforts have already either failed or are taking too long. Fires should either be lit in safe buildings (warehouses, concrete or brick lined buildings, etc) away from flammable materials, in small back alleys, or in metal barrels when they can be found. Do not light a fire around flammable materials such as wooden buildings or vehicles (oil and gas could ignite).

How to build: Fires should be built using smaller and more flammable materials on the bottom and stacking larger materials on top. Lint from dryers, paper material, and some clothing can make great tinder to initially get a fire lit. These items should go on the very bottom. Wooden furniture and other larger items can be added on top of the tinder in an orderly way in order to enlarge the fire. It is very important to note two things: air flow is needed for fire and some materials will burn and create toxic smoke. Both of these things coincide to make one important thing: Have as much air flow and ventilation as possible around the fire. Smoke inhalation, toxic smoke, and heat can all become problems in closed environment. The construction of the fire should be done in a way to allow air flow to the larger materials and to allow smoke to exit the general area.

How to light: There are a slew of ways to light a fire. In urban areas, the number of ways gets even larger due to the presence of tools and flammable materials. Lighters and matches are, of course, the easiest ways to accomplish this. If flint and steel was brought, they can be used as well. Some of the more esoteric methods of lighting fires that are used in wilderness areas such as rubbing sticks or creating bows will not be necessary or even possible in most urban areas. Lighting a fire is simple: just light the tinder on the bottle and blow a bit on it if necessary to create extra heat and air flow. The fire, if built properly, should grow to the desired size. If using a flint and steel to create a spark, it may be necessary to add some flammable liquid to the tinder such as a small amount of gasoline or high proof alcohol.

How to maintain: Maintenance of a fire is easy. This is particularly true in urban environments. Simply add fuel to the fire and keep the coals stoked in order to maintain air flow. The only issue with fire maintenance is making sure that none of the surrounding environment catches on fire. This is especially true in areas that may be carpeted or have other flammable materials (such as wood floors or low ceilings).

Water purification – The need for water has already been established. But the question is: what does a person do when their clean water has run out? How can a person replenish their water supplies in an urban environment that is probably full of water, most of which is very likely contaminated and unsafe to drink? The answer is: purify that unclean water and make it drinkable.

Purification tablets – These can be used easily to purify water. The package should have the exact instructions for use. The steps vary between types of tablets.

Boiling – This can be done either through the use of fire or through the use of some sort of electric heater if possible. Simply put the contaminated water into a pot capable of being heated and heat the water until it boils. Boil for five or so minutes and then allow to cool. The water should be safe to drink. This method will destroy bacteria and pathogens that may be within the water.

Collection – During times of rain, water can be collected in buckets and cups. Assuming there has not been a radioactive event, this water should be safe to drink immediately, but there is always an added safety measure that can be added by boiling the rainwater before use. Urban environments often provide hundreds of vessels in which water can be collected. Much more than would ever be found in the wilderness. This is not, however, to say that stagnant pools of water found around the city will be clean. Only trust water that has been personally collected.

Principles of good shelter – Shelter can be as simple as something to keep rain off of the survivor. Shelter is one of the great benefits of being in an urban area. Almost any building can act as a shelter. They can protect from the elements as well as providing a bit of safety from marauders or predators. When choosing a shelter make sure the structure is stable and safe from flooding. Make sure the area chosen is not already inhabited.

How to handle weapons – Practice at a shooting range can solve this problem. All of the weapons in the world will be of no use to a person who does not know how to properly use them. This would include weapon maintenance, cleaning, and storage. Good gun maintenance can prevent misfires, can help maintain aim, and can prevent other problems associated with dirty or damaged firearms.

How to signal for help – Urban environments provide an array of possible options for signaling help. Sound tends to carry and echo in urban areas because of the high density of buildings. Small radios can be used to receive or transmit signals from other survivors or from rescuers.

Flares are another possible option if they are available.

Smoke signals will probably not be much use in an urban setting. The reasoning is simple: anything burning will probably be making black smoke making it very difficult to discern smoke signals from actual fires. In addition, unpredictable wind directions and obstructed view from buildings makes smoke signals virtually useless in urban environments.

Signals can be left on walls of buildings or on the ground with chalk, paint, or permanent marker. These signals can either be left to lead rescuers to the location of survivors, to designate safe areas and safe directions for others to go in. Signals can be as simple as SOS, HELP, X, or arrows. There are, in some cases, established protocols for the types of signals to leave. One of the problems is: even if a prepper knows these signals, the average person won't. The best signals to leave are simple signals that indicate something and are easily interpreted.

Sunlight – Sunlight can be reflected off of CDs or mirrors or any other type of reflective surface. Sunlight can make an effective signal even over relatively long distances. The density of buildings within urban areas may make this form of signaling less effective than it would be otherwise. This is especially true when the amount of metal and glass objects in urban areas is considered.

First aid – Of the priorities in a first aid situation, they go in a specific order: restore and maintain breathing/heartbeat, stop bleeding, protect wounds and burns, immobilize fractures, treat shock. It is extremely important that, before approaching an accident victim, you check for danger to yourself and insulate yourself from it. Electrical cables, wreckage, unstable structures, gas pipes, or falling debris.

One of the first things to do when administering first aid is to remove the victim from danger. The rule is to move from danger first if possible and then to administer first aid.

If breathing but unconscious, turn the victim on their side so that any blood or vomit does not choke them should they spit up.

If alone, the Heimlich maneuver can be self-administered by pulling or pushing against some sort of blunt object like a tree stump, a chair, or something similar.

Arterial bleeding is the most dangerous kind of bleeding. If a tourniquet cannot be applied and nothing is available to stem the bleeding, the bleeding can be slowed by applying pressure to the appropriate pressure point. It would pay dividends to any prepper to memorize the major pressure points of the body in case of emergency.

Getting Rescued

Getting rescued can be a situation unto itself. As with all other survival situations, getting rescued should be the number one priority after survival itself. This can occur in one of two ways: either the prepper must remain in his or her home until help comes and things return to normal or that is not possible and the prepper must leave the home along with his go bag and anything he or she might need and go find rescue. Most of the preparation for staying in the home should already be done. Food and water should be accounted for. Home defense and route planning should already be done. With all of these things taken care of, the only remaining scenario that needs to be accounted for it finding help.

With route in hand and the go-bag prepared, all one needs to do to begin finding help is to simply leave the home and go to where help might be found. The hand-crank radio should be used in order to listen for signals from rescue crews. Look for signals when on the road. Avoid risk and be safe, but look for written signals in chalk or paint that may lead to an enclave of survivors or help. Be amicable with rescuers if they are found. Avoid carrying weapons in the open if searching for help.

Final Thoughts

Prepping is not difficult. Prepping in an urban environment is not difficult. Urban prepping simply requires a different set of skills, knowledge, and items in order to accomplish its goals. One should not be afraid of the unknowns that come along with a disaster. The primary goal is to be as prepared as possible for the slew of contingencies that may come along with survival situations. Food, water, and shelter are the most important things to have during a survival situation. A good route and a little pre-planning can ensure that all of the items necessary for survival are already in place before a situation occurs.

The higher population and the density of buildings in urban areas brings with it a slew of hazards and situations that will not be encountered in rural or wilderness areas. Disease and insects are able to thrive in urban areas. Insects, in particular, can form dense populations in the crevices that urban areas provide. Particularly with the presence of human waste and the plentiful sources of water that are available in them. It is important to know that knowledge and experience go hand in hand. In any survival situation, it is better to err on the side of caution and not to take risks unless absolutely necessary. This is particularly important in urban environments where there is increased risk due to population and building density.

As with any survival situation, staying put is the first best option. If a person must leave due to a mandatory evacuation effort or because the home is compromised, a route should be pre-planned for leaving the urban area. Once out of the home territory, all efforts should be made to survive and to be rescued. This may mean having to find the way to a safe area on foot or finding some means to signal a rescue effort. Good route planning and a map will help greatly with the effort to find rescue.

Proper preparation for urban survival can ensure a safe journey through a disaster. Being prepared can help both the prepper and his or her family remain alive during a moderate to long-term survival situation. Urban survival provides unique challenges that are not present in rural areas. Wilderness challenges are replaced with urban jungle that must be overcome by those choosing to live in those environments. Urban prepping is a subject that is both simple and complex at the same time. Be safe, don't take unnecessary risks, stay calm, and remember the basics. Knowing these rules and following them will be the difference between your family surviving and prospering or not.

Good luck!

*****

If you've enjoyed this book, please consider leaving a review and sharing your opinion with others.

Sign up for Robert's Mailing List to be notified of **New Releases** and **Special Sales**: http://eepurl.com/zvm11

No Spam – he promises!

Other Books by Robert Paine:
The Ultimate Prepper Collection: Survival Guides For Every Situation
Prepper's Pantry: A Survival Food Guide
The Survivalist Cookbook - Recipes for Preppers
Prepping 101: A Beginner's Survival Guide
The Dead Road: The Complete Collection

www.ingramcontent.com/pod-product-compliance
Lightning Source LLC
Chambersburg PA
CBHW070639290526
45790CB00001B/143